ELAINE

READ MY LIPS

RHETORIC AND THE
POWER OF PERSUASION

SNACKA SNYGGT

(TRANSLATED FROM THE SWEDISH)

Published by
LID Publishing Ltd.
The Record Hall, Studio 204,
16-16a Baldwins Gardens,
London EC1N 7RJ, United Kingdom

31 West 34th Street, 8th Floor, Suite 8004,
New York, NY 10001, US

info@lidpublishing.com
www.lidpublishing.com

A member of:

BPR
Business Publishers Roundtable

www.businesspublishersroundtable.com

Printed in Great Britain by TJ International
ISBN: 978-1-911498-43-8

Cover and page design: Caroline Li

ELAINE EKSVÄRD

READ MY LIPS

RHETORIC AND THE POWER OF PERSUASION

LONDON   MONTERREY
MADRID   SHANGHAI
MEXICO CITY   BOGOTA
NEW YORK   BUENOS AIRES
BARCELONA   SAN FRANCISCO

Contents

Introduction

Martin Luther King, with his 'I Have a Dream' speech, has been widely considered the best rhetorician of all time. People have tried to emulate his style and manner for half a century now, but with limited success. That's because King was very much a man of his time. Today, we listen to things differently. There have been many books published in which rhetoric is situated firmly behind the speaker's podium, but here we want to make it useful in your everyday life.

The purpose here is not to try and magically transform you into a Martin Luther King or a Barack Obama, but to help you become the best version of yourself in terms of communicating, motivating and persuading. Is this possible, you might wonder? Of course it is! If you haven't figured out how to do that, I guarantee that this book will help take you there.

First and foremost, rhetoric is not something that's just for politicians or actors. When I comment on rhetoric in the media, it is often about the rhetoric that I like the least – the sort that stays firmly planted behind the speaker's podium. I am often asked, 'Who is the best rhetorician among the politicians?' That is roughly like asking, 'Which sumo-wrestler runs fastest?' Politicians today are not so fantastically skilful. They do things that completely deaden one's motivation for listening. They have a speaker's podium and a printed script or teleprompters that they mechanically read from. But surely, you might think, they *must* have to do it that way. My response to that is, 'Who says so?' Not us rhetoricians at any rate.

Let us go back to King's 1963 "I Have a Dream" speech. Contrary to popular opinion, it was actually a deadly boring speech. At least that was the assessment of gospel music legend Mahalia Jackson, who was sitting in the front row. While King went on and on with his written remarks, more than a few listeners could be seen yawning. Half way through the speech, Mahalia shouted out, "Tell us about the dream, Martin!" King stopped short, looking out at Jackson and at the sea of people standing there listening to him. He took a deep breath and did something that many politicians, and communicators in general, could make great use of. He literally improvised what would become one of the most iconic proclamations in history – 'I Have a Dream!' He spoke from the heart and shared what he had envisioned in his inner-most dreams.

When I emphasize positive models among rhetoricians, I usually look to the ranks of professional speakers, because they are paid to talk. The best I have heard so far are the photographer Mattias Klum and Professor Hans Rosling. And because they are so good they are two of the best paid in the industry. Rosling tops the field, and he talks about… statistics! Can you imagine that there are people who pay hundreds of thousands of kronor to listen to a subject like statistics? That is some consolation for the rest of us, because if his starting point is to get people to listen to statistics, then we have a very good starting point. I have lectured together with Rosling on several occasions and every time I have noted that he is just the same up on stage as he is afterward. On one occasion I asked him if he behaved differently when he was on stage and when he was with his family. "There is no difference at all; it drives my family crazy," he said with a laugh. Then he told me that his dream had originally been to become an actor. "But my teacher in drama class said that I was hopeless. The only person you can portray, Hans, is you yourself!'"

His failure to become an actor was in fact a stroke of luck for him as a communicator. From that point forward, he only had to be himself. Most people find it extremely difficult to be themselves when they step onto a stage, give a talk or try to negotiate a pay raise. In Sweden we wear a heavy professional overcoat. When we are out shopping, phone customer service, talk with the bank and engage in most other everyday situations, few of us talk in an everyday way. Rather, there is a surfeit of professionalism and it's always quite robotic. In the US, however, it is understood that we don't trust people who are too stiff and professional – we trust those who are personal.

This book will help you to present yourself as both professional *and* personal, without being too private. Your listeners, in turn, will become more interested and motivated, and that will make speaking more comfortable and fun for you.

There is no right or wrong in rhetoric. I am not going to re-mould you in some 'rhetorical model' where you should stand in a certain way or talk 'in a rhetorical way'. We shall find you your very own model. You'll still be you, but you'll be armed with a helpful array of rhetorical skills and techniques. Regardless of whether you are afraid of speaking in public or are a monologue monster who talks too much, we are going to help make you the best rhetorical version of you.

How shall we get there? I do not want you to immediately visualise yourself on a stage in front of 300 people. Even though that may be the objective for some of you who read this book, we are going to start somewhere completely different. We'll begin at the place where you feel that you can be 100% yourself, and preferably with an 'audience' that you can be yourself in front of. You will have an opportunity to choose that entirely on your own. But choose properly, because this will be the mental place you return to every time you want people to listen. It can be your favourite bar with your best friend, or perhaps a garden on a summer's day with your mother. Let's choose the bar. Imagine that you're sitting there with your best friend and you have each ordered a beer. The sun is shining, pleasant music is flowing from the speakers and the atmosphere can't be beat. You are going to tell your friend something. How would you do that in this sort of setting? Do you look for a speaker's podium? No, that would of course break the spell. Perhaps the situation calls for a PowerPoint or a printed script. *Seriously? Are you mad?*

You might argue that delivering a professional presentation is a far cry from telling your friend something over a beer. I agree that there is a difference, but just because a PowerPoint is boring in a bar doesn't automatically make it compelling in a presentation. It is a misnomer that certain rules of communication apply when you do a presentation, and others apply in everyday life. Most people don't want to listen to a presenter who articulates in a stiff, formal manner – they want to listen to a person, and that person is *you*. That is why it is important that you don't lose yourself and become that professional cyborg when faced with a rhetorical challenge. Think back to that bar and reflect upon how you would talk then and there.

There were approximately 300 of us sitting in a dark hall, waiting for a rhetorician. The spotlights lit the empty stage. Five minutes to go. We sat in silence and wondered how the speaker would manage to grab our attention.

In came the speaker. Half of his body was turned towards the audience and he walked with slow steps towards the middle of the stage. During those few short seconds we sat and analysed how he was dressed, sizing up which 'flock' he belonged to. All that I can remember is that he didn't fly with the Versace flock, but must have run with an intellectual crowd that didn't care much about appearances. And then he turned towards us, show-ing his face. The mouths of everybody in the audience dropped slightly; it was not a pleasant sight. The man had a scar across his face. His clothes were no longer of any interest. My inner voice asked, 'How did he get that scar?' The question repeated itself in my head like a mantra. The man studied our collective body language – 300 question marks arrayed in front of him. He had seen it before. How do you make yourself comfortable when faced with 300 question marks? And would he be able to silence our inner voices and pave the way for the message he hoped to deliver?

He raised his hand, but we looked at his scar. In the periphery I saw that he held up his index finger, but I was still looking at the scar. Then he slowly ran his finger along the scar. We followed it with our eyes as he said, "I got this in a car accident, 1973. My name is Janne." You could have heard a pin drop. This was ten years ago and I still remember his name.

Rhetoric is not the art of speaking – it is the art of getting others to listen. Most people can speak, but the art of getting people to *want* to listen is a skill with roots in antiquity. Rhetoric is when your pulse quickens as someone speaks. It is when certain phrases for some reason go straight to your heart and make your hair stand on end. It is when the subtleties of communication (voice level, body language, clothes, presence) are in perfect harmony with the message. It is these communication signals that we rhetorical consultants try to put our finger on and teach to those who want to acquire the power of words.

Other books have been written on the subject of rhetoric, but this one is different. There are a few things I specifically *don't* want it to be about. It does not deal with the history of rhetoric – not that it is uninteresting, but because it's been done before. Nor is it a book that teaches you how to *talk prettily*, as many people might think when they hear the word 'rhetoric'. Rather, it will teach you to speak effectively… and that, dear reader, will lead to lots of pleasant consequences. What if you could get people to listen to you all the time, in every situation? And what if you could get them to *want* to listen? Wouldn't that make life easier? Definitely!

As a rhetorician, making use of academic concepts can serve its purpose, but making oneself understood serves a higher purpose. You don't need to worry about excessive academic terminology. For those readers who are drawn to academic concepts, there is a glossary at the end of the book. There is no rhetorical value in verbalizing them, but you can keep their meaning in mind to help you speak more effectively!

If a listener leaves you with the impression that you're smart, then you are smart. If a listener quotes the words you said, then you are a rhetorician. You will get people to understand you, but beyond that, you will get them to *feel* what you say. Nelson Mandela once said , "If you talk to a man in a language he understands, it will go to his head. If you talk to him in his language, it will go to his heart."

The objective is to master the art of getting others to listen to you, plant your words in their heads and also get them to quote you. People with power almost always have the power of words – one rarely goes without the other. This book is not just for those who are competent in a skill or discipline and want to learn how to convey their knowledge more effectively. It is also for those who want to see through empty words, manipulators and incompetent people, and be ready with the retort, "I see what you're trying to do, but you don't fool me."

You will get to learn how to give a classic speech so that people want to listen to you, to handle your nerves and communicate with various personality types. As I have already mentioned, there is not just one correct way to speak, but various different ways. When you gain insight into the various personality types – as well as which type you yourself are – it will be easier to find new ways to communicate. People have long thought that rhetoric is only for extroverts, but more than a third of the world's population can be characterized as introverts, and that is in fact one of the better starting points from which to develop rhetorically. You will find out how in the chapter *Monologue monster or low-key charisma? The art of communicating with different personality types*.

Incidentally, this is a new & improved version of the first edition of *Snacka Snyggt*. You could say that it is the best version. The first one was good, but this is much better. More practical tips, and timeless examples that you can make use of whenever you need them, regardless of whether you are giving a speech at a wedding, negotiating a pay raise, or offering criticism in just the right way. Modern rhetoric is rhetoric cross-fertilised with psychology, so you'll come across some psychological theory in these pages, and it should prove enormously helpful to you.

Chapter

1

Monologue monsters or low-key charisma? The art of communicating with different personality types

I remember my first day at school. I was seven and about to start my first class at Bredäng School in Stockholm, Sweden. I was really looking forward to it and walked proudly to my classroom. It was a big day and I felt grown-up. As we prepared ourselves, we sat in a circle, with the teacher in the middle, and I was so curious about my classmates. What surprised me was that almost all of them whispered their names a little shyly. I, who came from an extroverted Brazilian-Swedish family with (by Swedish standards) loudmouthed friends from Haiti, understood nothing. I had never seen that sort of behaviour before. I leaned forward to hear what my classmates said, and my teacher Carola told me in a friendly tone to sit down. When it was finally my turn to introduce myself, I stood up and shouted: "My name is ELAINE BERGQVIST." They all looked at me with wide eyes and I remember Carola saying, "But Elaine…" I took it as a compliment that everybody had heard me, but in that context it was not the best way to communicate with my new classmates. I was the extrovert among introverts.

It can be easy to think that there is something wrong with you if your style of communication doesn't suit the context. But this chapter will help you to understand that quite often it's not about right or wrong, but about differences. And when you learn how to identify what sort of rhetoric is suitable, then you will easily be able to adapt yourself to the situation using the tools you're going to get here.

We live in a society where a huge emphasis has been placed on social media. These days it's 'in' to be an extrovert, to be visible, to be heard and to have an exciting, colourful life on Facebook. It is said that social competence is more important than education. I agree that social competence is important, but simplifying that to mean that being extrovert is what's most important would be getting it all wrong. So if, as you hold this book in your hands, you feel that you don't want to be seen and heard all the time, that is perfectly alright. It is important to point out that there is not a right or wrong here; we are simply different. And a lot depends on the context, but regardless of whether you like talking a lot or a little, the idea is to get people to want to listen when you do choose to talk. People who walk into a room and get everyone's attention are said to be charismatic. Less is said about those who perhaps don't get everyone's attention straight away, those with low-key charisma and a less tangible presence who don't necessarily aspire to being seen. The extrovert and introvert personality types are fine in different ways, and the book starts with this particular chapter since it is good to keep this in mind as you read on. When the objective is to inspire, there is more to it than simply being an extrovert. Introverts should be aware that they don't need to change their essential nature to inspire others; sometimes being introverted can be a gift in that regard.

Regardless of whether you like standing at the centre of things and speaking in public or if you prefer to talk a little more pro-foundly with one person at a time, you are going to get people to want to listen. All of us have both extrovert and introvert sides to our character – we variously like to be on our own, or like to be with others, on different occasions.

The purpose of this chapter is to get you to calibrate the com-munication to the level that's most appreciated by the person you are talking to. Many people make the mistake of talking to others as they themselves want to be talked to. That's the wrong approach; talk to them in the way *they* want to be talked to. So, here you are going to learn how to formulate one and the same message to be addressed to four different personality types.

Introvert or extrovert
- how to know which sort you really are

It was Swiss psychiatrist Carl Gustav Jung, the father of analyti-cal psychology, who was first to divide people into extrovert and introvert personality types. He characterized them as individuals for whom personal energy either flows outwards or inwards.

The quickest answer to which type you are is provided by the question, "Do you have a need for solitude or the company of others?" But some people belong in the third category, alternately craving company and time alone – they're called ambiverts. Biologically speaking, the difference between being extroverted and introverted is the degree of activity that is necessary for your hormones to tell your brain that it is satisfied. For introverts, not much outside stimulus is required to be satisfied. In other words, they can sit on their own in the woods for a long, quiet afternoon and like it. The journalist Therese Bohman, herself an introvert, has written about precisely this:

> "One of my finest childhood memories is from when I was per-haps four years old and sat next to some dog-rose bushes by the roadside on the street where I grew up. It was summer and nice weather and I poked in the sand where the asphalt ended and grass and bushes took over. I sat there quite a long time. Nothing happened at all."

Introverts appreciate the warm-up before a party more than the party itself, they prefer a few close relationships rather than many casual ones, they think before they speak and don't regard silence as uncomfortable but as calming and pleasant. What makes introverts the bolder type, in their own way, is that they don't need to belong to a group. They dare to be by themselves and dare to stand up for a cause by themselves. As an extrovert, I look on with astonished admiration. Of course, I can stand up for things, but when I do I like to have a whole crowd standing there with me.

Introverts are often passionate under the surface, and inde-pendent thinkers, free from anxiety and the need to try and please everyone else. Their existence does not depend on a crowd of people thinking the same as them; being alone is in other words not frightening but entirely desirable. Jung thought it natural for extroverts to generally be most interested in their introverted side from age 30 to 35. Introverts don't make that journey so late in life – since childhood they've been forced to live in an outside world that they may have viewed as shallow. So being an introvert is not a diagnosis, it is a completely normal personality type that fits every third person. That means there are a lot of them out there, and there will be times when you will want them to listen.

One thing that was clear to me early on as an extrovert is that the response from an introvert is not as fast as from an extrovert. Why? It's because introverts think before they speak and we extroverts talk to be able to think. Do you recognise yourself as someone who talks to a technical appliance while you mess around with it? "Come on, you little devil, now we'll get you to work." That is a typical characteristic with extroverts; they need to hear their thoughts to be able to move on with what they are doing. That is why what we extroverts say is not always thought through. Rather we can take things back, reformulate and start again, perhaps three times in short order. And while we are doing that, the introvert is standing there, silently having this dialogue *inside their head* instead of in their mouth. I have learned that when my husband actually says something it happens perhaps ten seconds later than it would have if I had been talking, even though he thought first. Another thing that has struck me is that an introvert can process what I have said over the course of a whole week and then phone me and say, "Elaine, I've been thinking about what you said last week and have decided that…" That provides me with an enormous dose of good feelings. As an extrovert, I could hardly be happier than when I've been at the centre of somebody's thoughts and reflections for an entire week!

Extroverts feel more comfortable with new acquaintances; they like to start conversations and turn strangers into friends. They become more easily restless and they do more to get dopamine kicks. They look for new meetings, places and experiences, and take greater risks to achieve them. They become energetic and efficient under stress. The natural enemy of the extrovert is an empty diary, while that of the introvert is the telephone that interrupts and surprises with intimacy. Extroverts wear their reasoning on the outside, while introverts keep it tucked away on the inside. Introverts, in other words, mull over their problems just as much as extroverts but they do it inside their heads, and don't make a pronouncement to those around them until they've come to a conclusion.

An introvert is: silent, observant, has a flow of energy that goes inwards, focuses in depth, is confidential, reserved, reflective, thoughtful and cautious.

An extrovert is: talkative, involved, has a flow of energy that goes outwards, focuses widely, is social, enthusiastic, and has energy and drive.

Rhetoric: When you talk to a particular personality type it helps to think about how your rhetoric matches the descriptions above. When you as an introvert talk with an extrovert, it can be worthwhile to put forth a bit of extra effort. And when you as an extrovert talk with an introvert, think for a moment so that the other person doesn't have three different formulations to try and sort through. The introvert does not want to follow your line of thinking, but wants to hear a well-ordered conclusion that is a *result* of your thinking process.

Thinking and feeling

Jung also distinguished between how thinking and feeling people worked through the decision process. Thinking people are more rational in their thought process; they like what is measurable and factual. They don't ask, 'What was the party like?' They're more inclined to ask what actually happened at the party. If you ask a thinking person, it's perfectly appropriate to describe it without evaluating the events emotionally. For them, things should preferably take place systematically, following a logical, sequential plan and structure. Entering a restaurant and being given a menu is for the thinking person (and presumably for most people) exactly how things should be. But if, the moment they walk through the door, a waiter were to appear and ask, "What do you feel like eating?" they might wonder if he was out of his mind.

A feeling person does not count the number of guests at the party but gauges the mood. This is a person who convinces others with *pathos* (the fine art of emotional persuasion). They can find it difficult to convince *logos* people (thinking people) with arguments such as, 'I feel...'. The thinking person might think it is nice that you 'feel' but for them it is preferable that you tell it like it actually is.

I remember a lecture I attended that was scheduled for 13.00 – 16.00 hours. The audience was very engaged and the lecturer was the 'feeling' type. At 16.10, with the program running past the scheduled end time, I (a thinking person) was irritated that he hadn't stuck to the timetable. And then the lecturer suddenly said, "It's ten past four... but what do you say? Shall we go on?" The audience, which was a feeling crowd, delightfully exclaimed, 'Yes!' I sat there quietly fuming until I demonstratively got up and left. Feeling people are extremely flexible, sometimes to the detriment of others who lead highly structured lives.

When you communicate with these two types, you should bear in mind that they like different sorts of rhetoric. If I have a thinking audience, I always tell them how I have structured the lecture or course. They get to see a bulleted PowerPoint agenda with the times for breaks, lunch, start and finish. That is enormously appreciated. Feeling people don't pay much attention to that slide, but nor do they feel aggrieved if I do show it. If I don't show it to the thinking audience, it is roughly like that waiter telling his patrons, "We don't have a menu."

Sensation or intuition

For the third personality type parameter, Jung had as his starting point how we take in and deal with information from the world around us, via sensation or intuition.

Sensation here means that which is measurable and tangible, here-and-now facts. Sensation-oriented people express themselves very precisely. When faced with new ideas they rely on previous knowledge and experience, and examine a new idea on the basis of that. For them, development often takes place by gradually developing what they already have. These people are often seen by their opposites (unjustly, I might add) as reactionaries who are unwilling to embrace change. But they are happy to change when they become fully aware of what is to be done and when they see that change as justified. It is good to know that, when you present an innovative idea to somebody who is the sensation type, a critical response does not necessarily mean they think you're daft, but quite simply that the idea ought to be based on their past experience.

The intuitive type prefers to see the world in wider terms. They readily express themselves with phrases like 'roughly speaking' and 'on the whole'. They are not as precise and exacting as the sensation people – decimal points and carefully plotted-out schedules just aren't as important to them. If you are intuitive, then you find it hard to stay focused when facts and figures are presented to you. An Excel spreadsheet full of figures will immediately make you jittery. To hold the interest of an intuitive person and keep them inspired, it helps to lay out the general picture, so that they can create their own context and start visualizing implications and possibilities. Since intuitive types don't tend to devote themselves to routine work, they on the other hand often welcome changes large and small.

To reach sensation people you should be: Specific, focused on the here & now, realistic, consistent, down-to-earth, practical, precise, factual, step-by-step.

To reach intuitive people you should be: Global, looking to the future, imaginative, unpredictable, dreamy, conceptual, general, abstract, spontaneous.

How will you know who is what!?

With that brief primer on personality types, you'll surely know which describes you best. But how do you know what other people are? I shall now go through the colours, based on Jung's parameters, that will help you recognise various personality types. Discerning them in the people you meet will require different sorts of techniques.

There are various techniques and methodologies used to combine these parameters so that they can be synthesized and assessed on the fly. For instance, the Myers-Briggs Type Indicator, a widely used psychological assessment, utilizes combinations of letters. Someone is classified as ES if they're an extrovert and a sensing/sensation type.

Alternately, the Insights Discovery system uses a colour-coded wheel to categorize a person's style, needs and expectations. An extrovert and sensation type is designated sunshine yellow, for example. Insights Discovery uses this approach because the brain finds it easy to remember colours – you can visualize the pie chart as you encounter people in your day-to-day life. You will soon get a feel for whether a person is fiery red, earth green, sunshine yellow or cool blue.

Philosophers and thinkers since the ancient Greeks have suggested that, on various levels, we all have colour energies inside us. Before we start, you should know this maps to the three personality type parameters. Fiery red and earth green personalities are farthest from each other in terms of interpersonal communication style. Likewise, cool blue and sunshine yellow are complementary/opposite colours.

Fiery red personalities

Fiery red personalities are extroverts and thinking types. These people are primarily interested in **results**. You never need to work out what a fiery red person thinks; they'll let you know. They tell it like it is and don't dress it up in lots of arcane rhetorical formulations. If they want to talk to you they simply say, "We need to talk, ring me in five minutes!" Another colour would get a headache from that sort of blunt proposition, but for a red person it is simply a matter of getting right to the point. They just want to be efficient.

This is the person who gets irritated and sighs out loud in the queue to the salad buffet if the person in front of them pauses to think about whether they should take tomatoes or cucumber, or perhaps a bit of both. That thinking time can be irritating for a red person. Why not simply try the tomato or the cuke? If you want the other one later, just go back and help yourself… but don't hold up the rest of us.

That is the reason why a red person never reads instruction manuals when they buy some technical apparatus or a piece of furniture that needs to be assembled. They simply get on with it, and do what seems best. What a red person says is 'efficient' somebody else can say is 'too fast and simply wrong'. But a red person doesn't see any major problems with a few mistakes; those can always be rectified.

Signs that you're talking to a red person: The person is formal, uses direct formulations, looks you straight in the eye and is clearly focused on the objective. If you are sitting in a meeting and something unexpected happens, the red person might not even notice, not because they are arrogant but because they are focused on the objective. They exhibit a sort of tunnel vision. The person talks and answers quickly and has a direct manner of speaking. They are also focused on the task, and are generally challenging and pragmatic.

Rhetoric that appeals to a red person: 'I'll deal with this quickly', 'This will only take a minute, at most', 'To put it bluntly' and 'This is how it is'. All choices of words that indicate that everything will be dealt with as quickly as possible and that you are results-oriented – these will have the red person wrapped around your little finger.

Avoid: Things that totally kill the red person's motivation to listen are formulations such as 'To take this from the beginning', 'This might take a while', 'We'll deal with this when it crops up', 'I'll take this slowly so you'll understand' and 'I feel…' To hesitate, babble, try to take over, be emotional or simply waste time should be avoided with the red person.

Earth green personality types

An earth green person is introverted and feeling. They are the direct opposite of the red types. Their primary goal is **harmony** and with the confrontational reds that can feel virtually impossible. If you want to know what a green thinks, don't expect them to tell you spontaneously. Ask them instead. This person doesn't demand space but is quite happy to be one of the crowd. If a green gets a phone call from a telemarketer they can calmly listen to the salesman for fifteen minutes only to then say that they aren't interested. A red says so from the very beginning, but a green doesn't think there is cause to be unpleasant. They don't make sweeping gestures, but have a more low-key rhetoric. Being at the centre of attention just isn't a part of their nature. The green is often afraid of conflict – a natural consequence of liking harmony. The problem in green working environments and other social contexts is that conflicts can hang in the air for years because nobody dares to deal with them. A green person is a really good team player, while the reds prefer to go solo if that strikes them as more effective.

If you are going to talk to a green, you need to be careful with your rhetoric. Being blunt can be fatal when it comes to the green. Instead of saying, "You did wrong", you ought to formulate yourself in terms like, "It feels as if there are things we could work on here". Such a change in the formulation often makes all the difference as to whether a message lands or not.

A green has many qualities, such as being willing to cooperate, friendly, calm, stable, loyal, good at listening, obliging and considerate. But a red can interpret that behaviour as ineffective, since the green always strives to let everybody have a say so everyone *feels* good. The red thinks that we simply must reach our goal, and if someone gets trampled underfoot along the way, that isn't such a big deal.

Signs that you're talking to a green person: A sort of low-key friendliness, a limited degree of eye contact and very few gestures. The person is investigative, has a gentle tone and a slower tempo, because they want everybody to be on board. They are considerate, easy to be with, a bit cautious and ready to cooperate. In working situations the red is the person who keeps the group together, and in the family they are the negotiator.

Rhetoric that appeals to a green: 'How does this feel to you?', 'It is good if everybody can have their say', 'It's going to be nice' and 'We'll take this at a steady pace so that everyone can keep up'. Ask them for their opinion, take things slowly, be patient, give them time and be diplomatic.

Avoid: Pushing through quick decisions, surprising them or using & abusing their friendliness.

Sunshine yellow personalities

Sunshine yellow types are extroverted and feeling. Their primary goal is **attention**. They are the direct opposite of the blues, referred to below, but they have some things in common with the greens and reds. They are extroverted like the reds and feeling like the greens. They are that sociable colleague who always wants to talk, not just to tell you something but sometimes purely to hear their own voice. They don't laugh just because it's funny, but also so that people will hear them laugh, and they can laugh that little bit extra when everybody else has finished laughing. A yellow sneezes with an especially long 'shooo' and loudly thanks the person who says, "bless you!". The yellows are those colleagues you always notice as soon as they enter a room. A green likes to blend in somewhat discreetly; a yellow wants to be the sun that blazes into the room and is impossible to miss. It could be that stranger who sits next to you on the train and reacts out-loud to an email that they are reading, even though it has nothing to do with you. The person demonstratively nods their head whilst listening to music in their headphones. They always let you know that they are present, and sometimes that can be tiring for the other colours.

Yellows are spontaneous and flexible, they're constantly soaking up impressions of what's going on around them, and as such they can easily lose track during an ongoing dialogue. A colleague told me that it was especially apparent that she was yellow and her husband red when they were out running. He told her, 'I'm concentrating on getting to the end of the track all the time, but you can come up with ideas like abandoning our run to go for a spontaneous swim. Besides, you run faster when we have an audience.'

Yellows like social events and things should preferably be fun, and formulated with superlatives – otherwise they easily lose focus.

Signs that you're talking to a yellow person: They are social, flexible, engaging and informal. The person is talkative, spontaneous, expressive and lively. It is not unusual for them to gesticulate a lot; it increases their chance of being seen. If you don't look at them, it might lead to physical contact so that they can get your attention.

Rhetoric that appeals to a yellow: Here it isn't primarily the formulations that count, but rather that you always actively include the yellow person. Otherwise, they might wander and start thinking of something else. Inspiring and enthusiastic rhetoric appeals to these people, and you should be generous with your superlatives.

My husband is blue and I am yellow. After a lecture by Tony Blair I asked him what he thought. He was silent for a few moments and then answered, "It was good". As a yellow it is rarely just 'good'. Add an 'extremely' in front of every formulation and you'll get our attention. Other formulations that work are: 'Flexible', 'We'll deal with it when it comes', 'We'll have to feel what it's like' and 'It's going to be fun'.

Avoid: Getting bogged down in details, doing presentations as Excel spreadsheets or talking about routines.

Cool blue personality types

Cool blue types are introverted and thinking. They are the direct opposite of yellows but are introverted like the greens and thinking like the reds. The primary goal for the blues is to **understand**. They can ask lots of questions to achieve that goal and because of that they are seen as being critical. That is the eternal misfortune of the blues. So if you are a blue you should always try to adopt an inquisitive rhetorical tone where you tell people that your purpose is not to criticise but to understand. A blue may want you to go through the agenda in detail again just to make sure that they haven't missed something. They are the ones who read (or at any rate skim through) the instructions when they've bought some furniture or a technical apparatus. Quick and wrong is not their style; one can do it correctly from the start.

Sometimes I hold 'Blue Rhetoric Courses', where I adapt the contents so that they will suit blue course participants. Engineers tend to be a group that prefer this. On the second day they are given the task of delivering a three-minute presentation, the objective of which is to arouse goodwill, curiosity and credibility. Those three words often sound wishy-washy to blue people since they are not measurable. That is why they always ask the same question when they've finished the presentation: 'Was that three minutes?' In other words, measurability is the be-all and end-all if you ask a blue.

Signs that you're talking to a blue person. They are often low-key and like to observe, and when they speak they do so without sweeping gestures or physical contact. Since they strive for factual information they have little variation in their voices. In their striving to understand they will ask questions, take in your answers and quietly think, since the information is being processed internally, as opposed to how the yellows do it. A blue person is formal, controlled and to some degree reserved.

Rhetoric that appeals to a blue: Never forget the details when you talk with a blue, or they will think you are careless. 'Now, if we look at the details', 'Let's start again from the beginning', 'The facts tell us', 'What is relevant here'. Artificial pauses should not be underrated; a blue does not think that silence is unpleasant. On the contrary, a blue sees it as a sign that what you are saying has been thought through. Be wary of over-evaluating events; describe objectively what has happened so that the blues can arrive at their own conclusion.

Avoid: Really, steer clear of everything that to other types is desirable when you are talking to a blue! If you answer too quickly you will give the impression of not having properly thought it through. If you use very sweeping gestures or superlatives, then a blue can dismiss you as unserious and exaggerated. A blue is a person who doesn't want to hear that something is fantastic, they want to hear about the process that leads to the inescapable conclusion that it's fantastic.

How do I get people to want to listen if they are a different colour than me?

First and foremost it is a good idea to make use of this colour filter when you look at the people around you and their style of communication. If you don't click with a person, it doesn't necessarily mean that you or they are communicating badly, but just differently. But remember that to some degree you have access to all the colours inside you. If you as a yellow meet a blue, then you should think about toning down the yellow, and turning up the blue instead. I usually do that when I'm talking to my husband and take longer pauses when he asks me something. He doesn't want to hear my three different variants of an answer that I revise while I'm talking, he just wants to hear the final version. It doesn't matter that it takes a little time before I get there, even though that delay would drive me crazy if I was the listener. But, essentially, you shouldn't speak to people in the way you want to be spoken to, but in the way *they* want to be spoken to. That is the basic rule.

You who read this book and feel that you are blue or green, in other words the introverted personality types, remember that a large part of the world's population are like you and actually think that your communication is appealing. There is a great misunderstanding about only the yellows being good communicators; there are also many introvert communicators who have inspired with their low-key charisma. Gandhi is perhaps the best example. But Rosa Parks, Albert Einstein, Charles Darwin, Eleanor Roosevelt, J.K. Rowling and Steven Speilberg are also good examples. These people – thanks to their introverted nature, will to understand and ability to observe – have achieved a great deal, but what was (or is) their rhetoric like? Really excellent in its own way. Good rhetoric comprises both extroverted and introverted communication.

To be inspiring is not synonymous with being a yellow personality. It is about doing something more than what is expected of you. If a professor starts to talk about the journey of his life when the subject is statistics, it becomes inspiring because it is unexpected. A yellow person can inspire, by using strategic silence for once, that too will be unexpected and will make it more interesting. But the most important of all is that when you communicate with other colours and turn up the level of one of them inside yourself, it should still remain fairly true to who you are as a person. After all, you want to be the best rhetorical version of yourself – not of somebody else.

To develop your rhetoric to its maximum, it is important that you study models that you can relate to in style and expression; it will then be easier for you to approach them. I am a yellow and I often look at personalities like the talk-show host Ellen DeGeneres, but even if I have her as a rhetorical model it is not impossible for me to be inspired by a speech by Gandhi or some other introvert. On the contrary, many times extroverts can be driven crazy by other extroverts. They're often drawn to their opposites, choosing to marry an introvert, for example.

Remember that you can communicate with other colours as long as you bear in mind that there are things that can cause a head-on collision. So the next time you come to the conclusion that the chemistry's not between you and somebody else, you can turn up or tone down the colour necessary to work better with the other person.

Bear this colour-thinking in mind as you read the book, and then we will be well on the way to finding your best rhetorical version in various situations.

Chapter

Five steps to get the listener's attention

Before you say anything, you should be aware that regardless of the situation you are in, the people around you will first and foremost notice what you look like. Your chances of success are affected by what you look like and by the context. This is not necessarily because people are prejudiced, it is associated with how the brain functions and allows us to work through everyday life – it sorts information and generalises. The generalising effect means, for example, that we can come to the conclusion that the chair is a chair in a fraction of a second. But this ability can, regrettably, be a handicap when we look at people. We think we know what they can and can't do, whether they are nice or not so nice… simply by looking at them.

Your appearance matters, and it matters a lot. It communicates an abundance of information, and what it communicates depends entirely on where you are. But we shouldn't be downhearted because people might get the wrong idea about us. Rather, we should put physical appearances into perspective so that we are one step ahead of these preconceptions. And not only that, we have an opportunity to turn these preconceptions into advantages.

This can be done by: putting yourself into perspective; being wary of your own prejudices about your listeners' prejudices; planting positive notions of yourself in the listener's mind without overtly spelling them out.

1. Put yourself into perspective

This first part can be done in three stages: put yourself into perspective in terms of outward appearance, position and social factors. Let's start with physical appearance and why it is so important.

The psychologist Karl Rydberg claims that it only takes a third of second for the reptilian brain – the part of us that processes sensory input at the most primitive, instinctual level – to reach an initial conclusion about a new person. These conclusions are drawn to a great degree from basic appearance – not necessarily clothes, but rather your genetic foundation: black, white, woman, man, older, younger, and so on.

Some people totally miss this part, and that can mean that their message gets lost on its way to the listeners. Why? They are too busy with what they are thinking about you. Janne, described in the previous chapter, had done his homework. He knew that people would think about his scar, so he addressed it right at the beginning. By mentioning his scar, we could to a large extent forget about his appearance and start listening to what he had to say.

You should do the same. Now, perhaps you don't have a scar on your face, but you might have another sort of 'scar' that everybody is aware of. Perhaps you are a woman in a male-dominated context, or vice versa. Should you then say, 'Hello, I am a woman'? Absolutely not. Instead, it is about confronting things that they might be thinking about you. And how would you know what that might be? Read *The Art of Mind-Reading*? No, all joking aside, you might actually consider asking people what they thought the first time they saw you, when they only had your outward appearance to go on. Gaining that sort of insight will give you an advantage. Don't miss the chance to do so.

First of all gain an understanding of the context and the communication situation (*intellectio*), and then put yourself in context. You are, after all, not an observer – you are the messenger. Another important rule is that the message should be adjusted to the audience (*aptus*).

Ask a number of others what sort of person they thought you were the first time they saw you. It is important that you tell them to be brutally honest. Flattery won't get you very far; you want to know what people think, regardless of whether it is good or bad. But remember that you don't want comments that appraise your appearance in terms of good-looking or slim, but what sort of person they thought you were.

Recall those assessments the next time you are going to try and persuade a listener. If they are to your disadvantage, then play them down. If they're to your advantage, then they are self-evident and you don't need to mention them, since the basic impression you give speaks for itself. The trick then is to twist their prejudices into advantages. And you do that by calling upon examples and experiences you've had that prove the opposite.

Beware of prejudices about your listener's prejudices

Forget your generalisations about the audience. They won't help you to get people to listen. What you should be interested in are the listener's prejudices *about you*. That is the key to grabbing their attention. Their preconceived ideas about you are, after all, your enemy, if they don't say the 'right' things. 'Right' is of course a relative term, but if the listener's thoughts don't match who you are, then you certainly ought to take them into account. Of course it isn't so easy to know what somebody else is thinking; you risk having 'prejudices about prejudices'. But reflecting on others' perceptions of you will get you far. If you are standing in front of an unknown listener, think about widely held societal values and prejudices. Let's say that you are blonde, a woman, and young (or older). What ideas does that arouse in the listener, at first glance, right then and there?

Place yourself, mentally, in front of the people you are going to talk to and imagine what sort of ideas your presence will arouse. Janne put himself into perspective, and that was the key to getting us to listen. In that case, his physical appearance stuck out so much that we couldn't focus on what he said until he'd dealt with what we saw.

Janne inspired me so greatly that I felt challenged to do exactly the same thing, to meet the audience at my outmost border – my shell. I did that precisely by asking acquaintances and customers what they thought the first time they saw me. The most frequent comments were that I was 'young', 'tall' and spoke 'good Swedish' (it was the elder generations that made the last comment). I decided to retain 'young'. That worked until the day I stood at the front of a school hall filled with sixth-form students. They weren't quite as wide-eyed as we were when Janne stood in front of us, but nevertheless I wanted to talk about my appearance.

"A lot of you here are wondering, 'Is she a teacher or a student?'" You could hear a pin drop. The students looked inquisitively at me; some of them smiled and I felt that I had them in my rhetorical grasp.

"And one or two of you might be thinking, 'Gosh she's sooo young!'" I went on dramatically, but was suddenly cut off by a handful of students who said, "No way!". A painful lesson that is worth remembering: not everybody thinks the same. My mistake was that I hadn't put myself into context, mentally, first.

When you know what the prejudices are, you can turn them to your advantage. But how do you go about working that magic?

Plant advantages - don't name them

A lot of people make the mistake of listing their advantages. Instead, you ought to plant the values in your listeners with the help of argument. Don't say: 'I am socially competent.' Instead, tell them about situations you've been in that will lead the listener to come to that conclusion. Provide examples that make the desired conclusion inescapable. There are those who would argue that you should list your triumphs and describe yourself with lots of superlatives. They would lead with, "I am very open and engaging and have a great sense of humour." Such a comment can, perhaps, be good for your self-esteem. But I am a rhetoric consultant and my job is not to improve your self-esteem. I'm here to teach you how to get people to listen to you. Listing advantages will get you part of the way there, but not far enough. Instead, plant a sense of who you are, but don't articulate it in so many words. Keep it short and sweet: think about your fully visible disadvantages, and disprove them. Think about your advantages and subtly introduce them.

There are many examples of famous people who have obviously pondered, worked through and thoughtfully addressed the prejudices and generalisations other people likely have of them and their outer shells.

When Barack Obama was a candidate for the American presidency, he and his rhetoric consultants knew that he would arouse powerful reactions in the voting public. Preconceived notions included a sense that he would primarily have the interests of African-Americans in mind. The challenge was to turn those prejudices into advantages. Never before have we heard a presidential candidate talk so much about his background and his genetic makeup. It would be historic – an unprecedented milestone – for an African-American to become president. But it would also pose a whole host of challenges in an America that was still quite segregated. What could have been a handicap, he turned into an advantage. Obama emphasized his seemingly obvious disadvantage in such a way that he took ownership of the right to represent huge segments of the population. He emphasized the other half of his genetic background that wasn't so obvious to the naked eye – the white part. And if he hadn't had that, he might have had to trot out the old, 'I have a good friend who is white'. But he didn't need to do that, because he had his mother.

"I am the son of a black man from Kenya and a white woman from Kansas." "I've gone to some of the best schools in America and I've lived in one of the world's poorest nations." "I am married to a black American who carries within her the blood of slaves and slave owners – an inheritance we pass on to our two precious daughters." "It's a story that hasn't made me the most conventional of candidates, but it is a story that has seared into my genetic makeup the idea that this nation is more than the sum of its parts – that out of many, we are truly one." (From Obama's speech *A More Perfect Union*, 18 March, 2008.)

What makes Obama, and other great rhetoricians, succeed in the art of getting people to listen is that they meet the listeners and their notions head-on.

If you are a woman *and* young, then say what everyone sees – that you are a young woman. But also make clear what is not seen, that you have competence. Make visible that which can't be seen with the naked eye. Then your listeners will stop wondering. In Sweden, we are extremely obsessed with age, and listeners won't stop thinking about me in that respect until I mention my age. 'I'm 29 years old' can make the lecture better, or worse, depending on which preconceived ideas they have about that particular age. Then I tell them what I have done, and that often trumps the prejudices they may have about that age group.

What is positive about seeing yourself from the perspective of the listener is that you show that you can look at yourself objectively. Your self-distance creates closeness because you are indirectly saying, 'I am like you because I see what you see'. That makes the listener favourably inclined (*benevolus*) towards you. But it is important not to be paralysed by all the possible negative generalisations that exist about your demographic. Don't turn those generalisations into your 'truths'. If you do that, then fear will creep into your soul, and grow, and turn into stage fright. When you have put yourself into perspective, you should leverage the advantages of being (for example) a young woman to win over your listeners. Twist the perspective around, from that of the listeners to your own, as Obama did when he mentioned his mother.

We can learn from Obama when we take rhetoric down from the speaker's podium and out into everyday life. I had a client who was 26 years old and a midwife. She told me that the hardest thing for her was to give a credible impression in her field of work. "The midwives who have the most credibility are those who are older than 65," she said, clearly dejected. In other words, she had done her homework and put herself into perspective, so she knew that what was negative about her appearance was that she was not in her 60s. It is important that you don't stop there, when the situation can seem hopeless. Rather, that's when you must press on and give people reason to think otherwise. I asked her how many babies she had helped deliver. "Two hundred, perhaps," she answered. For somebody who may not be knowledgeable about the subject, that sounded like a lot of experience. I would have felt safe with somebody who had assisted in 200 deliveries. So I encouraged her to introduce herself with her name and how many deliveries she had assisted with – something like, "Hello, my name is Lisa, and I've assisted at 200 deliveries so you can feel confident and safe." The midwife liked my suggestion but had one little objection: "The midwives who are older than 65 would certainly have assisted at more than 40,000 deliveries." I agreed that she shouldn't mention that; you simply have to be selective in what you inform people about.

But the midwife found a way to make herself credible despite her relatively young age, and you will have to find a way to make yourself credible. Sometimes you will find yourself in situations where it is more credible to be a woman, while in others it's better to be a man. But don't feel sorry for yourself. Instead, find a way that makes you credible.

Your professional title or position in the context

Something else to think about when you try to put yourself into perspective, in a given context, is your professional position and title. Are there any generalisations held by people about your title, be it chartered accountant or father? For example, I know that many salesmen have to deal with preconceived notions and prejudices when they say what they do for a living. And I, as a rhetorician, often encounter the misunderstanding that we work with manipulation. The most important thing in such situations is not to get angry. Never go into a rant, saying something like, "You obviously don't get it. What a pity for *you*." Nothing could be more wrong. If people haven't understood what you told them about yourself, one shouldn't pity them, it is you who should be pitied. That's your problem. After graduating and becoming a professional rhetoric consultant, I soon realised that people didn't understand what that really meant. I heard an awful lot of off-base questions. "Are you going to give a speech on Speakers' Corner?" "Are you going to be an actress?" It didn't take me long to translate my title into something that most people could relate to: "I give people tools to enable them to get others to listen to them!" Whatever your chosen profession, you can do that too.

If your title is complicated – like, for example, 'key account manager' – then figure out how to say in simple terms what that means in practice. What do you actually do on a day-to-day basis? What difference does your job make for the people to whom you provided goods or services? If you are a salesman, perhaps you can translate your job description into helping people to find the perfect car, or financial management software, or whatever it is you sell.

Simply put: present yourself with a brief, easily-understood definition of your title, instead of the title itself.

People who know you
- what impression do they have of you?

Finally, you should put yourself into perspective socially. Since the aim is to become the best rhetorical version of yourself, it is a good idea to have a realistic grasp of how others see you. "But that depends on who I ask," you might be thinking. And that's right, so you should ask several people.

This exercise is usually rather unpleasant initially, but extremely exciting and profitable after just a minute or two. You should choose a family member, a friend or a colleague to phone. And you should then ask them two questions:

1. How would you describe my personality?
2. What can I do to grow and develop?

It is of utmost importance that you get an answer to that second question; remember that it is your task to make them feel sufficiently comfortable to be able to answer it truthfully. When you've gotten the answers, you will have gained an advantage in having persuaded people you know to tell you what you're asking about. It is easier to adapt your rhetoric and – for instance, to make it more attractive and humble – if the answer you got to question two is, "You are sometimes too pushy."

A good friend tried to persuade his live-in partner that they should buy a ticket to South Africa a whole year before their planned travel dates. To his partner, my friend was known to be the feeling type who rarely thought logically. And so, practical suggestions he might offer rarely fell on good soil. Aware of this, he used credibility reinforcement (ethos reinforcement). He reinforced his credibility by quoting a person whom his partner viewed as quite credible. So he said that his friend, David – whom they both regarded as a very logical, organized person – had suggested that they buy the ticket a year in advance. Since the message came from somebody she had faith in (her partner was only the messenger) she listened.

Use your clothes strategically

When you now have managed to get the better of what you can't change about yourself – your genetic makeup – it is time to see what you can control in a way that can steer people's thoughts. Namely, your clothes. It is not about being fashion conscious; it is about being aware that clothing speak and getting it to say exactly what you want it to say.

From now on, I want you to think tactically every time you open your wardrobe. And the strategy should go further than just making sure you look nice and smart. A lot of people think about dressing to look great. They obsess over having a designer necktie or – even worse – getting into that (too small) size again. During my rhetoric courses I have seen the latter result in open zips and blouses with peepholes. One thing characterises such blunders: the message you're trying to deliver is obliterated by the apparel mistakes. What you are wearing should never distract from what you are saying. You clothes should strengthen your position, your message, your values… and they should create closeness to the listener. If you have made an impression *for real*, then your attire isn't going to be what the audience remembers. Ideally, they should forget what you were wearing. And to make sure they don't focus on your clothes, we are now going to direct our focus on precisely that – clothes.

An effect well documented by psychological research is called the law of representativeness. It seems that people have a tendency to come to conclusions about a phenomenon based on it being experienced as representative of the type. Let's say you meet someone who wears baggy, stained clothes. With matted hair and red eyes. The first information that reaches you is immediately run through the memory bank you have of what type of person this outward appearance represents. Is the clothing representative of a dentist? A bank official? Or for somebody who sleeps on park benches and digs for food in dustbins? My guess is that the individual in front of you would best match the average understanding of what a homeless person looks like. The clothes represent that type more closely than the others. What happens is that you immediately start to assume that the person has qualities that (based on your experience and values) are representative of that category?

You have pre-conceived ideas – like we all do – which can lead to crazy scenarios. Here is one such storyline:

I sat in the first class carriage on the train to Nyköping, a city in south-western Sweden. Suddenly two elderly gentlemen come into the carriage. "First class all the way home, so everything is as it should be," one of them noted happily and then gave a surprised glance in my direction before taking his seat. During the entire journey, he continued to look at me. I ignored him. He just seemed slightly curious. I am accustomed to travelling first class more or less every day, with men in business suits who notice me but don't say anything. Suddenly the train stopped, and the man who had stared the longest got up. He looked worried and studied my afro hairstyle before exclaiming, "Is this really first class? Are

YOU travelling first class?!" The whole carriage held its breath. My jaw dropped. Did he really say what I thought I just heard? His comment sounded more like something from 1910 than 2010. I couldn't help but answer, "For heaven's sake! How does it look like I'm travelling? By horse and cart?!" A swell of laughter rose up from the other suits in the carriage. It may have been the Twenty First Century, but not everyone had apparently been on the same journey through time. For that elderly man, at least, I represented somebody who does not travel first class.

My old grandfather, born in the 1920s, explained it simply for me. "But my little friend, it was because you have your negro hair. You ought to straighten it like you usually do."

That is the effect of representativeness. And what people's conceptions are depends on which country – or which decade – they were born in.

It is because of this effect that your choice of clothes will set off various thought processes in the people you meet. And within a few seconds they will have formed an impression of you, based purely on what your clothing and appearance tell them about where you belong and the type of person you are. Do not underestimate this!

I once trained a managing director in rhetoric and he wanted me to skip all the stuff about clothes. He told me, "I don't care about such shallow things!" The problem is that people must be able to look past the surface to reach the depth of your message, and if you haven't thought about your clothes, the surface can stop them before they have a chance to listen. The unpleasant task for which the managing director was preparing was to announce that 40% of his company's workforce would lose their jobs. We structured his message, but it never reached the intended audience because of an unfortunate miscalculation regarding his attire. The day he was going to inform his employees that the company was in grave financial trouble, he had put on a heavy Rolex wristwatch, which, to put it mildly, smacked the workers in the face. When you want your message to get through to people, sink in and truly resonate, you can't afford to make a mistake with what you wear.

In everyday life we all communicate through our clothing. Some people do so with expensive designer clothes, from top to toe. What is their message? They are signalling that expensive, prestigious garb is important for them. Others dress down – comfortable old shoes, oversize trousers and a shirt from 1992. They want to show that they aren't interested in fashion. At the same time, they may also be telling us that they choose to focus on inner qualities. Whether you elect to get all dressed up or to dress down, your clothes will communicate.

When I lecture it is exactly the same. The audience draw their initial conclusions on the basis of my attire. If I don't have any accessories – just a scarf around my neck, jeans and an everyday top – I'm automatically seen as 'Left Party'. That may be because I've been known to wear a scarf that resembles the Palestinian keffiyeh shawl, which western youth adopted as a sign of opposition to Israel in the 1970s. The dynamic is so ridiculously simple that I can wear green-coloured clothes and the audience will conclude, 'Environmental Party'. But they're not consciously aware of why they think that until I ask them. Think about your message. Make sure your clothes strengthen that message. (And no, my choice of clothes for the pictures in this book does not indicate any particular political affiliation. I just thought they looked nice.)

I usually talk about four clothing strategies: values strategy, position strategy, closeness strategy and message strategy. If you first ask yourself what you want to achieve, it will be easier to choose your clothing strategy.

Values strategy

Your clothes hint at your values. What values do you want to be associated with? Think about that, and choose your clothes accordingly. It is not entirely easy, since people see apparel in different ways. But you need to think about the context, what your clothes signify in that particular setting, and how that fits in with your message.

Some companies have thought a great deal about the link between values and clothes. One client of mine, we'll call him Thomas, was going to meet the director of an IKEA store. He stood waiting by the main entrance. A man came out and Thomas thought he was a maintenance man or possibly an 'ordinary' IKEA employee. The man looked just like all the other employees – the same yellow/blue outfit with the IKEA logo on his chest and a name tag. And yet the man standing in front of him was the director of the store. Thomas never forgets that meeting, and the company's philosophy of 'everybody being equal' sank in. The strategy is well thought through – a moment into this encounter Thomas had a firm grasp of the company's values and character. And the only tool the store director had used was his clothes. He is not alone.

Perhaps you want to look like a computer nerd, or a person who's committed to environmental issues. There are certain *looks* that people associate with different values, personas and professions. Think what perceptions different clothes are associated with, and choose an outfit that suits who you are and how you want to present yourself.

Message strategy

It was a chaotic world where people looked for those responsible for all the poverty and misery. The economy had tricked them. The bottom had fallen out of everything. Would things ever get better? What had happened to the security and prosperity they had previously lived with?

In that time and place, slogans such as 'change' and 'yes we can' just wouldn't have fit. Instead, a man stepped boldly forward, time after time, and made himself heard. His clothes didn't hint at disruptive change. Rather, they signalled stability, continuity, security.

The clothes always looked the same. And he saw the frustration of the people and played to it with expansively dramatic body language. His words made them straighten their backs. Towards the end of his speeches they held their hands up in the air and chanted, "Heil Hitler!" Hitler talked about a Germany as it had been, and spoke of what it could again become. He didn't say "yes we can," he said, "I can." And he had the *right* clothes, the *right* body language and the *right* words – at the right time. Clothes can have enormous power when you use them to strengthen your message.

"The great masses," he said, "will find it easier to fall victim to a big lie than to a small one."

Just think if Hitler had used his rhetoric for something good! What remarkable changes he could have brought about. Reflect on that for a moment and think of others with unsound views who might be abusing rhetoric today. Keep a sceptical eye – and ear – on them! A bit later in this book you will find tools to help you see through them.

Here's another, completely different example. I was one of the speakers at the 'Big Day for Employees' conference at the concert hall in Göteborg, Sweden's second-largest city. I was sitting in the audience waiting for the first speaker – the inspirational speaker Claes Schmidt, who was appearing as his alter ego Sara Lund. Out onto the stage came a tall man wearing a dashing red leather skirt, a white blouse and high heels. His wig was blond, his lipstick red and his voice deep. The audience stared in fascination. There stood a man 'dressed up' as a woman on the stage in front of 400 people. Everybody had a slight smile on their face, perhaps because we thought it looked rather fanciful, or because we were glad that we weren't in his place. Little did I know that I was just about to hear one of the best lectures I've ever heard, and that the man dressed as a woman was to become one of Sweden's best rhetoricians.

She – as he was that day – started by telling us that she was a transvestite, which meant he was a man who likes women's clothes, not necessarily other men. Sara Lund was happily married to Anna and had been for 20 years. She took a few steps forward towards the audience in her high heels:

"My wife came home early from work one day and I hadn't had time to hide away my secret hobby. She found a pair of tights of a brand she never uses. There was a smell of perfume in the bed, and she found women's clothes here and there," Sara told us while we held our breath.

"And then my wife thought: *Claes must be a transvestite!*" said Sara with a wry smile. He was kidding, of course. Anna hadn't thought that at all. She assumed, as most people would, that her husband had been unfaithful. So there was only one alternative for Sara.

"From that day on, I came out as a transvestite."

Then Sara slowly but surely turned the audience's perspective to her own.

"I think it is so strange every time I am on a business trip to various places and meet these grey suits who all look the same on the flight. I once scrutinised my ticket to see if there was a dress code for flying. No, there wasn't, and yet they all dressed the same way. And who decides that?" Sara asked, in a concerned voice in her distinct Skåne accent (a Swedish dialect that many Swedes associate with Danish). I looked at Sara and at the dashing leather skirt. Then I looked at the people sitting close to me. Nobody stood out. We were a grey mass of 'ordinary types' who all melted together. Slowly, I began to feel more and more uncomfortable in my seat. Was it just a coincidence that the people in the audience all looked alike, or were we following some sort of unspoken dress code? Who decides how I should dress? We were dressed according to society's conceptions – the norm.

"The reason why transvestites attract such attention is not that we dress in the clothes of the 'opposite' sex – it is the fact that we break with the norm," Sara added.

My internal dialogue didn't stop there. Who decides who I am, which priorities I have and at which point I do various things? Is it me, or do *people's* reactions shape and drive what I do?

Sara's experience, as most of us will find in similar situations, was that anxiety over what other people will think is virtually always worse than how they really react. "Do you know what happened the first time I went out on the street as a transvestite? NOTHING!"

Sara's message was strengthened enormously because in her clothes lay a message that went far beyond LGBT issues. And the message reached every one of us in the audience. We could all relate to the 'transvestite'. But really, it wasn't about transvestism. It was about living your life as fully as possible. And what was so magical about the talk was that, in the beginning, she looked to be in disguise, but towards the end it was we in the audience who felt we were in disguise. She ended her talk with the words, "Are you living the life you want to live, or are you living the life you *think* that others want you to live?" That a man in a dress can get an entire audience to feel that they are in disguise, that is rhetoric on a high level indeed!

So, take another look in your wardrobe and see if you have any clothes you can use for the message strategy! Rest assured, you don't have to dress as a transvestite. Just make sure your clothes match your message.

Closeness strategy

If you want to create closeness to the person you are talking to, then you should dress like they are dressed. Subconsciously, your listener will generalise and think you have a lot in common. But – and this is a big 'but' – there are exceptions. If you are older and try to create closeness through clothing in front of a gang of young people, the effect can be tragically comical. Tragic for you, that is, and comical for the young people. The listener can take you to heart even if you look different. If you are the only lawyer in the room, then in that context your clothes ought to strengthen your position. Dressing like your listeners is not a smart move if you want to tell them that you know more, or have a job where a more formal dress code is generally known.

> *"If I turned round every time somebody called me a 'fairy' then I would have to walk backwards – and I don't want to walk backwards."* (Harvey Milk)

The American politician Harvey Milk was a humanist who struggled for the rights of homosexuals in 1970s San Francisco. At first he looked like a left-wing activist from 1968. He had long hair, with a ponytail, a beard, corduroy trousers and an open shirt. His goal was to be able to walk in the corridors of power, elbow-to-elbow with the suits. But there were some obstacles: Milk's sexuality and his clothes. Freedom of sexuality was what he was struggling for, so he couldn't give that up. So he took a page from George Orwell's novel *Animal Farm*. In that classic work, the animals struggle against the farmer for their rights. The pigs, who seize upon the power vacuum, gradually begin doing everything like the humans did. They put on clothes. They shake hands with each other. In the most powerful scene, at the end of the book, other animals stand outside a window and watch as the pigs negotiate with the humans. Hopefully waiting for their rights to be addressed, they see the pigs on all four feet dressed in their suits. Then, slowly, the pigs get up on to their back feet and the animals outside no longer see a difference between the pigs and the humans.

Harvey Milk put on a suit and nobody saw the difference between the 'homosexual man' and the men in suits. The clothes gave him a push – his garments now said, 'I look like you – so I am like you.' Milk climbed up through the hierarchy and made history. He became the first openly homosexual elected official in America. He managed to push through gay rights reforms before he was shot and killed by a politician rival in 1978. By then he had already gained a place in the hearts of the people, where he still lives on. In 2009, then-governor of California Arnold Schwarzenegger declared that May 22, Milk's birthday, should be dedicated to him. If you want to create closeness, dress like those who you want to listen to you.

Position strategy

A successful salesman revealed his greatest selling secret to me. He has climbed so high in his field that he no longer needs to sell, but along the way he had to deal with both rhetoric and what he wore. At the telephone shop where he worked, the dress code required a piqué shirt and a black waistcoat. Nobody bothered with the waistcoat. "So I made sure I always wore mine," he told me, and I was curious why. "Well," he said, "because when the customers saw me and my colleagues, I stuck out because I was dressed differently. They thought I was the boss, so they came to me instead of to the others." A smart move. The salesman signalled with his clothes that he held a position separate from the pack; he chose to stick out. He was indirectly saying that he knew something the rest of the staff didn't. The leader doesn't usually look the same as the rest of the flock since the group needs to be able to distinguish whom they're going to follow. The position strategy quite simply says that clothes should show your position in the relevant context. Steve Jobs used it. He didn't want to look like the other computer nerds; he cemented his position as leader of that flock in his iconic, every-day outfit of black mock-turtle-neck, faded jeans and worn-out athletic shoes.

So the question becomes, what do you want to communicate with your clothes? You can choose what you want, but choose cleverly. Dress like those you want to convince, but not too distant from who you are, and do it in a way that will stand the test of time. That way, you're saying, "I am almost like you, but with slightly 'better' views that I think you will eventually come to agree with." If you are a lawyer who wants to tell your clients, "I am a lawyer indeed, but here you can relax," then take off your jacket off undo one button on your shirt – no more. And, if you are a managing director and want your employees to listen but not ask questions, dress as much like a managing director as you can and fasten the top button of your shirt so that it is really tight. And then wrap it in a red necktie and pull it all even tighter. If you are going on a date and the message is, "Look at my *décolletage* all evening," then put on a low cut dress and you will be a success. But if the message instead is, "Get to know me and what I have inside my head," then you don't want your clothes too overtly sexy. Sex will come sooner or later. Use clothes strategically when it is time for precisely... that. (No clothes at all usually drives home such a message quite effectively.)

Study people with a similar message to yours. See what they're wearing. That is good, basic research for when you yourself want to be heard. But make sure you study those who are listened to, and not the others, the ones who dress wrongly and can't hold anyone's attention. Or, for that matter, study them as well so you'll know what *not* to do.

Different clothes give different impressions – choose right!

Values strategy - wear clothes that link you to the values you want to mirror.

Message strategy - Dress so that your clothes strengthen the message.

Closeness strategy - Dress like the listener.

Position strategy - Dress the way 'people like you' dress (for example, the way lawyers dress). Pick colours that arouse the right associations. Dress smartly, but also close to your personality so that you don't lose what's uniquely you and become a professional robot.

Use colours strategically

When you choose clothes there are four signal colours that you should be aware of. This is not connected with the colour filter, although the colours are the same: red, green, yellow and blue. The four colours have a considerable attention value. They're used around the world to deliver messages that are a matter of life and death: emergency exits, traffic signs, warning signs, protective equipment, apothecary and much more. If traffic signals had been codified in other colours, for example, there would be many more accidents.

Colour expert Karl Ryberg illuminates this point: "Colour is a language without words. Package the information so that the reptile brain understands. Colours speak to the reptile brain – before we spoke in languages, we could 'talk' colour. Add to your message with colour. What does the room look like? The colours should suit you. Don't dress in a colour that is theoretically correct, but doesn't suit you aesthetically. The reptile brain should approve the visual appearance; colours that inspire confidence should match the message. Proof-read your text, but also proof-read your colour."

The political parties of Sweden have chosen their colours strategically. The Moderate (Conservative) Party used to have royal blue, but interestingly changed to light blue because they wanted to portray themselves as the new workers' party. And then, of course, you can't be associated with royalty. But they couldn't be associated with the red side either. In a bid to attract working people they subtly adjusted the colour and wording. The new colour said, 'We are blue, but not as blue as we used to be, so you who are not extremely red can comfortably come over to our side.'

Look at me! - Colours that demand your attention

Red is a charged colour. It is a warning sign. Subconsciously, we associate red with blood and that makes us react. If we are sitting in a dark room and a camera flashes, our brain will register red as it fastens onto our retina. And that releases adrenalin into our bloodstream, signalling the primal *fight or flight* response, teetering between fear and aggression. Red also activates stress hormones, raising our pulse and body temperature and priming our muscles for action. Our pupils grow bigger. If you have a red bedroom and suffer from sleep problems, that's what might be causing them. Having said that, wearing red clothes won't make people want to hit you or run in the opposite direction when they see you coming. They will, however, notice you. Red arouses subtle feelings of fear. It is an effective colour to use strategically. Traffic warning signs always have a red element. When Obama gave a speech on the war in Afghanistan, he positioned himself as the war president. The colour of his necktie? Red, of course, as is often seen in the corridors of power. But it is important to distinguish between reaction and association. What our forefathers associated with blood has, over time, come to be associated with love and sexual charge.

Green is calmness and security

The colour green calms us. It gives us associations with nature and forests that soothe us and make us feel protected. Our reptile brain thus never sees green as dangerous, and that is one reason why in Sweden, for example, emergency exits are green. In the US, on the other hand, exit signs are red, which seems crazy. It would probably be hard for us to stop if we came to a green stop sign. Our association facility trumps the words, the message. People become calmer in green environments, muscle tension decreases and we move in a more relaxed manner. Our mood evens out. If you want to give somebody an unpleasant piece of information, then you should definitely choose a green room with down-to-earth colours to support a feeling of security. Staff rooms, rooms where you can lie down for a while, and clinics that deal with stress would benefit with elements of green. In operation theatres the surgeons most often have a green or a blue robe – imagine what it would be like if they were dressed in red instead. You would certainly find it much harder to relax.

Companies and products that want to be associated with being friendly to the environment often have a green logo, or brown to be connected with the soil. Products that are intended to fool the buyer into thinking they have chosen an environmentally friendly alternative might have green details. It is important to use colours strategically. But it is just as important to see through the people who use colours to manipulate you with a contradictory message.

Yellow - attention

Imagine that you are in a cinema with bright yellow seats. You would probably open your eyes wide and get an extra dose of energy. Yellow is the bright signal colour that our reptile brain associates with the sun. It is morning and time to get up. Our pupils become smaller and more focused, and we become more alert. Yellow gets our brain going. It is an excellent colour in forums for education, teaching, conference rooms and other contexts where you want the listeners to pay attention and be active. Research has shown that the reading skills of dyslexics increased when the text was written on yellow paper. Yellow can be seen from a distance. Many warning signs have yellow elements, or a yellow background combined with red or black. On traffic lights, yellow arrives to draw our attention to the fact that they will change in a moment to either green or red.

Speaking of traffic, Australian researchers examined the colours of vehicles that had been in 850,000 accidents involving at least two cars. It was a comprehensive project that spanned 20 years. They came to the conclusion that the colour of a car can clearly be linked to accident risk. White cars have long been regarded as the most visible and thereby the most safe. But if you want to minimise the risk of crashing into another vehicle, then you should choose the colour that makes us alert – yellow. The risk of accidents decreases by 1% if you choose a yellow car. That isn't so much, one might think. But if we compare them with other cars, yellow was the only colour that ended on the minus scale. If you choose a green car, you increase your risk of accident by 4%, and blue by 5%. With a black car it was up by 6% and – besides – the risk of having an accident with a black car at dawn/dusk was as much as 47% greater! In New York the taxis want to be seen, and it's hard to miss a yellow taxi.

Yellow and blue, just like red and green, are complementary colours and they strengthen each other. That is why the Chiquita label is blue – so that the bananas will look extra yellow and inviting for the buyer. If you want to strengthen these colours, you should have them next to each other.

The Swedish TV cook Fredric Andersson uses yellow in his kitchens. There are several reasons for that: "Yellow stands for happiness, joy, intellect and energy. The colour is also connected with food. It helps with quick thoughts and a clear analysis, and gives associations to the sun and gold. In other words, it is a damn good colour, if you want happy chefs who work with lots of energy," Fredric told me.

If we look at the business world and successful companies, the colour often harmonises with their brand label. If you are going to go and work out in a gym, it is hardly surprising that you will be more motivated by a chirpy colour.

Blue is calmness and harmony

Blue is the most beloved colour in the world. That could be because the planet is blue, and the sky and the sea. Light blue signals awakening. Dark blue, however, is lulling, calming and subduing. A 'sign of night' that says that it will soon be night. Time to sleep. Your pupils get smaller, your pulse slower, your muscles relax. The mental effect is that you slow down.

Colour researcher Professor Rikard Küller and his colleagues at the Lund College of Technology did an experiment some years ago where they painted two rooms – one all red and one all blue. They then had volunteers stay in the room for a couple of hours, during which time their brain activity was monitored. It transpired that the blue room had a calming effect on the volunteers, while the red room was energising and increased their productivity. According to Küller, a blue bedroom is good for somebody who has sleep problems but, on the other hand is devastating for your sex life. Besides, the colour – in too large doses – can lead to depression (just think of people having 'the blues'). In contrast to the colour red, blue has a cooling effect. Many people experience blue rooms as chilling.

You will certainly have noticed this in aeroplanes where most aspects of the environment work together to calm you. They're designed to dampen any worries you may have. The choice of colour for the seats and the cloths is often blue. That too is a strategy to get passengers to relax. Many uniforms are blue, such as on the police. 'Calm down, the police are here!' I would expect confidence in the police to drop if they had red uniforms. And an aeroplane with a red interior would stress the passengers. Use blue when you want to calm an agitated group at work, or a friend.

Metallic - success/health/money

Metallic colours have a high information value because we have respect for metals. In the animal world, shiny glowing animals elicit more respect in the flock. Metallic colours signify health, strength and aggression. They also give an impression of success and a love of money. What's so great about the metallic look is that all colours can have metallic elements. So, if you want to appear down-to-earth and successful, go with the brown metallic suit. What happens then is that a colour (brown) that has little information to convey is given a fancy treatment with an effect (metallic) that has a high information value.

Colours that have little information to convey

Brown – secure, down-to-earth, organic
A typical colour with little information. If you miss signs in traffic, they often have such colours. In many countries the sign that indicates a 'tourist attraction' is brown... which, if you think about it, is rather contradictory.

Grey – neutral and powerful
Grey is also a colour that conveys little information since it hasn't made much of a mark in nature. This colour is like the figure 0 in mathematics. It's not without meaning, but it's nothing in and of itself. But it becomes something in relation to others. If you want to be neutral and convey little information, then wear grey. Use this colour when you want to show objectivity.

Black – dangerous, forbidden, dirty and sad...
Black is also a colour with little information. Black-and-white signs are rarely found. And, if you do come across them, they often have a lower grade of information such as 'fast-food stall' or 'Pentecostal chapel'. Black stands for that which is dark and invisible. Black isn't really a 'proper' colour, it is a colour that absorbs everything, including light. It is the opposite of white, which is a mixture of all colours, and instead reflects all light.

White – irreproachable
One often sees famous people wearing white clothes during court hearings when they want to project themselves as innocent. When Michael Jackson was tried for sexual abuses in 2007, and his family accompanied him to court, they all wore white. So did a large number of his fans, who wanted to prove his innocence.

Other colours that have little information are: beige, olive, earth and moss tones.

The colours of your clothes really can affect people's attitude towards you. A woman I know who works at a public relations consultancy always finds that potential clients are benevolently disposed to her in some – for them – 'mysterious way'. She noted that the clients suddenly said that they felt that she understood them. And the reason was that the PR-woman had thought about absolutely everything, even colours. She revealed to me that she simply chose to dress in the same colours as the client's company logo. She had influenced them in a subconscious way with the help of strategic colour choices. Of course, the colours can't do the job by themselves, but they can give a push on the road to the right feeling. Say you work for the coffee firm Löfbergs Lila (with a distinct purple colour in their logo and product packaging) and a customer 'happens' to be wearing a discreet purple detail. Such a detail can help to build up a feeling of understanding – but subconsciously.

Check the list below for colours that harmonise with the feeling you want to convey.

Purpose	Solution
I want to be seen	Signal colours: Red, blue, yellow, green
I want to blend in	Colours with little information: Beige, brown, white, black, grey
I want to look successful	Metallic elements
I want to create security AND RECOGNITION	Colour combinations that the listener is familiar with

Colour chart	
Red = warning/charging	Green = calm/security
Yellow = alert/attention	Blue = slow down/harmony
Metallic = Success/health/money	
Brown = down-to-earth/secure/organic	Grey = neutral/powerful
Black = danger/forbidden/sorrow	White = irreproachable

Your clothes affect your rhetoric more than you might think. If you dress nicely you will feel more self-confident. You will straighten your posture and speak with more assurance.

You will, of course, just like me, have taken work-related calls when you've been sitting at home in some old leisure clothes. It feels somehow as if the person you are talking to can see you, even though that isn't possible. "Can I get back to you in five minutes?" I usually ask. Then I quickly change and phone them back. My rhetoric gets better and so does the conversation. So dress comfortably and you will feel comfortable. But don't go so far as to dress in your old leisure clothes if you want to sound professional. I strive to dress comfortably when I'm giving a lecture, and that has an enormous affect on my rhetoric. I give my best lectures dressed in jeans, Converse shoes and a comfortable jersey. But sometimes the dress code is fancy and then I notice how I become more 'feminine' in my movements, I straighten up more and talk differently.

Remember that there are cultural differences in colours. The colours that talk to your reptile brain are blue, red, yellow and green. Metallic also attracts attention. The other colours can have various cultural meanings depending on which country you are in.

Chapter

3

How to use your voice and body language strategically

Your voice is a powerful tool if you use it properly. When we who are listening have thought about your appearance and your clothes, we are waiting for you to say something so that we can get a *feeling* for who you are. We think we can get information about what a person is like just by listening to how they talk. If you talk quickly, without breathing, people will experience you as stressed and will probably feel stressed themselves. If you think about it, there will certainly be people you don't like, not because they are not sympathetic, but because you can't stand their voice. David Beckham, for example, is incredibly handsome until he starts to talk. So the question is, what do people think about your voice? Don't be alarmed; the good news is that you can change it.

I once trained a group of doctors at a large hospital in Stockholm. They were going to learn more about rhetoric and domination technique (also called master suppression technique). During the break one of them came up to me. He had been sitting silently the entire time and his facial expression looked rather indifferent. He started to talk and his voice was anything but dynamic or happy.

"This is very interesting, Elaine," he said in a gloomy voice.

I knew that he meant what he said. But I also understood that his rhetorical weakness was his voice. It sounded monotonous. It was a rhetorical 'wall' that shut out happy feelings, or any feelings at all. He went on:

"When I give my patients good diagnoses they react just as negatively as when they get bad ones," he said, surprised but just as monotonously.

I didn't have the heart to tell him the truth, in the same detail that I am writing it here. But of course his patients react like that, when he sounds like he is giving a eulogy at a funeral.

Try to see your voice as a remote control, which you use to convey your feelings – these must of course reflect the truth; we are not trying to manipulate. The buttons on your remote will be 'emotional', 'happy', 'sad', 'angry', 'matter-of-fact manner' and so on. It is important that you press the right button when you speak. The listener will automatically connect your voice to the feelings that the message rests on. We subconsciously look for the emotional level in a voice. And we also show our own commitment in what we say. If the commitment is to sound genuine, it is naturally good to have feeling behind what you say.

Dialects make a difference too. In the US, actors with an accent from the southern states often play the villains in films. An intellectual, or a technically gifted person, tends to get a British accent. Perhaps it's because they don't sound so emotional (it is easier to believe that a Brit talks in a down-to-earth manner and that a Frenchman speaks emotionally). Here in Sweden various dialects are more or less successful, depending on the context. A Norrland dialect inspires confidence. And perhaps it isn't so surprising that many telemarketing companies are located up in Norrland. A Göteborg dialect usually lands high in the top-ten list. I myself have one of the least appreciated dialects in Sweden – a Stockholm accent, another that sits near the bottom of the list and is seen as grumpy.

It is hard to do anything about your dialect. But it can be a good idea to say where you come from so that people stop wondering about that and instead start to listen to what you are saying. The same applies if you have a foreign accent. Tell me about it. The listener will find it easier to focus if you briefly describe where you come from.

Dialects and accents aside, now we shall make sure that your voice becomes your remote control, showing the emotion behind the words. But first you need to know how you press the buttons. You do that by using body language.

Convincing tone

The American TV star Oprah Winfrey has undoubtedly one of the most confidence-inspiring voices in modern times. Her body language helps her. At the beginning of her sentences she holds her head leaning slightly backwards. When she starts talking, her head sinks slowly, which gives emphasis. If you lower your head at the end of sentences your voice will follow along and help you to sound convincing. Oprah says: "This is very important for America." What if, instead, she had gone up in tone on the last word? Would that have sounded as credible? Test this yourself by going up in tone on the word marked in bold type: 'This is very important for **America**.' It is unlikely that Oprah would have become one of the world's most powerful people if she had talked like that, and the explanation is simple. If you end a sentence by going up in tone, it will sound like a question. It gives an unclear impression, especially if what you say is a declarative statement. The former co-leader of the Swedish Environmental Party, Maria Wetterstrand, is also skilful at going down in tone at the end of sentences. And she has long had high credibility among Swedish voters. Some people do the opposite – they always swing upward at the end of a sentence. You can test this yourself by saying every sentence according to the instructions below. Raise your eyebrows and head slightly and go *up in tone* on the words in bold:

"Hello, my name is Anders **Karlsson**, and I am going to talk about **rhetoric**. I think rhetoric is extremely **important** and I know that you are going to think that **too**."

Now we are going to do the opposite. Lower your head slightly and go *down in tone* when you read the bold words. This is what it sounds like when people convince you:

"Hello, my name is Anders **Karlsson**, and I am going to talk about **rhetoric**. I think rhetoric is extremely important and I know that you are going to think that **too**."

An important rule if you want to convince somebody is thus that you should go down in tone towards the end of a sentence. You make an 'audible full stop' (i.e., it can be heard). Musical pieces most often have a lower tone towards the end and that gives the listener a feeling that the piece will come to an end there. Even dog-owners know that their dog listens better if they say 'sit!' with a lower tone instead of a 'sit!' that goes up at the end.

Melody gives feeling to the message

There is a distinct difference when you just say something and when you really feel what you are saying. When you do the latter, it affects an important part of your vocal delivery – melody. A lot of people aim for a formal tone when they really want people to listen, but unfortunately that is the tone that makes us lose our listener motivation. I want to listen to the person but the formal tone turns into an iron curtain for the emotion and the possibility to feel the emotions that lie behind the message.

I was sitting on a plane on the way to New York when the steward came with the dinner trolley. There were four hours to go and my stomach almost sounded as loud as the engines. I was hungry. When the steward had put the tray in front of me, I quickly noticed that it was a meat dish.

"Excuse me. But I ticked 'vegetarian food' when I booked my ticket. I'm a vegetarian," I said, and smiled apologetically. The steward smiled back and said in a jolly voice with a really bouncy melody: "Unfortunately we don't have any vegetarian food on board."

I felt provoked, for two reasons. The message was negative, but the melody was positive and thus the feeling too was positive. In the context, it felt totally out of place. This meant that the entire communication became contradictory – about as credible as the word 'happy' over a picture of a grumpy person. The steward probably wanted to be nice and give the message a soft landing with his happy tone. But the effect was the opposite.

There are ways for you to control your melody and it is partly about controlling your body language. We'll do a rhetorical exercise here and now. We shall train your voice. Phone one of your friends, if you aren't sitting next to one now. (Otherwise you can do the exercise aloud for yourself.) Describe your surroundings with your ordinary voice. Describe what the setting looks like: the colour of the walls, or the houses or scenery around you. Now do exactly the same, with the same words, but with six different melodies. Do one at a time...

1. The sports commentator.
2. A declaration of love.
3. The newsreader on the TV news.
4. The evangelist pastor (hallelujah!).
5. Story time in a children's nursery.
6. The speaker at a funeral.

Did they all sound the same? If they did (which is unlikely!) then you didn't use your body language. Do the exercise again and gesticulate wildly and use facial expressions when you talk. Your voice won't be monotonous and your body language will be dynamic. Mean what you say this time.

I notice this so clearly when I give a lecture. On the days when I don't *feel* what I am talking about, the audience is not as influenced by my presentation. The key is to visualise what you are talking about. In that way your feelings and voice will immediately influence the listeners. It is as simple as that. To convey emotions you need to feel. But I can't always manage that. I remember a time when I was going to talk about my grandfather Arne, who had died. I tapped into my feelings, but that ended with me standing there in front of 200 people and crying. How did the public react? They started to cry too. It was no worse than that. But so that I won't cry at every lecture, I choose the occasions when I charge every word with full-blown emotion and those where 50% is enough. It's important that there is some amount of emotion, of feeling, in your words. The dose may vary, as long as it is there somewhere.

Tempo - get a feeling for the mood and follow the flow

How fast you talk actually affects the pulse of the listener. That is why people can be irritated by fast speakers – suddenly, for no apparent reason, they make you feel stressed. The listener breathes at the same time as you. If you forget to breathe, it will affect your listener. And it is difficult to feel relaxed if the person you are listening to talks like a sports commentator. Talk at a pace that fits the content and setting, and allows your listener to keep up. But don't talk too slowly either. That is just as stressful when you know what is coming, before it has been said, and you can't wait for the speaker to get there. There is no perfect speed. Try to get a reading on the mood of the room. Get a feeling for the tempo, and above all make sure you adapt your message. A lot of people think that Mark Levengood, the Finland-Swedish writer and programme leader, has a fantastic voice and a wonderful tempo, but that wouldn't work for a football match. Nor would a sports commentator be very effective leading a yoga session.

A voice can say, 'I understand you and you have every right to feel as you do,' by mirroring the listener's tonal level.

When there was a power cut in the block of flats where I live, I heard somebody banging on the lift doors. I ran up the pitch-black stairs to the sixth floor and discovered that my neighbour had had the misfortune to get stuck in the lift. To calm her, I talked like a yoga teacher. But that only made her more hysterical.

"I have phoned the emergency number and they are on their way. It won't take long," I said.

"I HAVEN'T TIME TO SIT HERE!" she roared.

"Calm down now, it will be alright."

"EASY FOR YOU TO SAY THAT. YOU'RE SITTING OUT THERE!"

"I KNOW. IT MUST BE BLOODY AWFUL STUCK IN THERE!" I called out, slightly hysterical, and then she turned quiet.

"No, but, it… it'll probably be OK. When did you say they're coming?" She had calmed down considerably. My voice had conveyed that I understood her.

So, to *talk with small letters when someone is shouting* doesn't work if you want to create an understanding, or get that person to listen to you. Get a feel for the mood and follow the flow.

Tempo has an enormous effect on how we act and is deliberately used in certain shops. If the shop-owner wants you to shop quickly, then the music will have a fast tempo. For some reason, then instead of just strolling around the shop you rush around. You feel stressed – or effective – depending on how you look at it. It is difficult to walk around slowly when you hear fast music (and that music can be lethal in a car). When IKEA closes, for example, marching-style music can be heard from the loudspeakers, compelling you to move more quickly towards the checkout area and exit. Later we shall deal in more detail with the influence of melodies.

Emphasize, emphasize, emphasize – strategically

If you want to hammer home your core message, you must master strategic emphasis, stressing certain words. This emphasizes your key concepts so that the listener will realise that they are important. You know that you have succeeded if your listener makes notes, or nods when you stress key concepts. A monotonous voice is unable to emphasize your core message. But you can practise this skill. Read the sentences below. Stress the word in bold type and lower your head slightly to show that the stress should be there. For extra effect you can insert a micro-pause after the word.

Rhetoric is the art of getting people to listen.
Rhetoric **is** the art of getting people to listen.
Rhetoric is **the** art of getting people to listen.
Rhetoric is the **art** of getting people to listen.

Rhetoric is the art **of** getting people to listen.
Rhetoric is the art of **getting** people to listen.
Rhetoric is the art of getting **people** to listen.
Rhetoric is the art of getting people **to** listen.
Rhetoric is the art of getting people to **listen**.

Depending on where you place the emphasis – which word you put the stress on – the sentence gets a totally different meaning. In some cases 'people' is central and in others it's the word 'listen'. Do you want to underline a figure, a name or perhaps a quote? Make sure you put the stress on that part and use two micro-pauses – one before and one after the strategic emphasis. If you want your listener to associate a positive or a negative value with the emphasis, then you should go up or down in tone when you stress the word(s). If you go up in tone, it will become positive, and down in tone will become negative. You can easily go up in tone by raising your eyebrows. Test by going through all the sentences again, but this time raising your eyebrows when you emphasize the word in bold type. You'll see what I mean.

A pause for effect ('rhetorical pause') - for the sake of your listener

Pauses are quite important. Don't forget to breathe – for the sake of your audience. It is in the pauses that the listener breathes and has a moment to relate what you have said to their own life. Give them the chance to do so. But these pauses shouldn't be too long, or you risk creating an embarrassing silence. You can use them partly to give yourself time for reflection, partly to give the listener time to think about what you have said. Pauses also increase your credibility. They make you look like a person who doesn't 'just talk', but also thinks now and then. Brilliant comedians are good at using pauses so that the public gets the point and laughs.

Voice models

In what context do you want to make progress? What do they sound like, the people who 'everybody' listens to? And how do they speak? Study them carefully and make them your voice models. I previously mentioned Hitler and Martin Luther King as examples of brilliant speakers in general. But it is important to know that they were brilliant in their particular context. You probably wouldn't take him too seriously if your boss shouted out loud, "I have a dream!" So stick to the great rhetoricians in your own field. Ignore the others – unless you want to make progress in some other field. You can even study those who never get listened to. How do they sound? Keep them at the back of your mind so that you don't make the same mistakes. A big voice trap that everybody should avoid is nervous laughter after your sentences. That takes away ALL credibility.

Think about:

Conviction - going down in tone at the end of the sentence
Melody - giving the words the right feeling with the right melody
Tempo - affecting the pulse of your listeners as they sync up with your tone and pacing
Strategic emphasis - steer attention to the words/figures that you want to emphasize. Negatively/positively charged emphasis
Pauses for effect - increase your credibility and give weight to the stressed words
Voice models - study people around you who get listened to, do what they do so that it suits you
Nervous laughter - avoid nervous laughter after sentences. This kills all credibility

Body language

Body language is the first language we inherently master. If you look at little children you will notice that they use their bodies all the time when they communicate, and their parents 'read' that. Babies are instinctive experts at harmonising their facial expressions with what they feel and want.

When we become convinced by somebody in the adult world, we can't always put our finger on why. We have forgotten our first language. But body language can weaken or strengthen your message; it can make you more or less convincing. And if you regard it as a tool, you will also be able to effectively strengthen your message. But you must *mean* what you are saying. You shouldn't just think it, you should also feel it. Here's another exercise. Say the following sentences out loud – with feeling:

'I don't want to go with you!'
'How nice it was to meet you!'
'I am not sure whether this was the right thing to do.'
'What time is it?'
'What's your job?'

You will presumably feel how the sentences make you look different. Say them again, but this time in front of a mirror. If you could see that the various sentences made you look different then you have a good chance of mastering the art of persuasion. If not, this chapter will help you. Remember that you were an expert on body language when you were a child. You simply have to find your way back to those skills.

The amount of body language you use isn't important - that fact that you use it is!

I am often asked how great a part of the overall communication experience consists of body language. There is no clear answer to that question. Some people say 80-90%, because some research shows that 90% of the impressions we take in are visual (i.e., Jacob Liberman in *Take off your Glasses and See*). Your eyes are instinctively attracted to a movement, so that you can register potential threats. So it is much easier for the listener to continue paying attention to somebody who is moving than to a talking statue.

Other researchers, for their part, say that it is more like 74%. Albert Mehrabian, a Professor of Psychology specialising in verbal and non-verbal communication, suggests there is a 7%-38%-55% rule for weighting the relative impact of words, tone of voice and body language. He assigned this weighting to three Vs: Vocal (7% importance), Verbal (38%) and Visual (55%). In short, the communication we *see* has the greatest impact.

It is difficult to scientifically prove how much of our communication is made up of body language. But it is not difficult to come to the conclusion that it matters – and matters a lot! My rhetoric colleague, Totte Löfström, often says, "If you use your body language the right way, it is 10% of communication; if you use it incorrectly it is 90%." If you say, "I love you", and simultaneously make an obscene gesture, your body language will even be 100%.

My point is that body language matters. How much depends on the context. When I appeared on the Swedish news programme *Aktuellt* and commented on the politician Mona Sahlin's body language in connection with the election campaign in 2010, I was criticised afterwards. A lot of complaints came from people who hadn't understood what rhetoric is. Some of them were of the opinion that facial expression and body language have nothing to do with rhetoric – that the words alone are what is important. Of course they are important, but if you make an obscene gesture and sound ironic while you make a declaration of love, then the non-verbal communication carries heavier weight. You don't need percentages to understand that.

The Greek philosopher Aristotle, the godfather of rhetoric, claimed that credibility (*pistis*) was not only built up with words but also by the actual presentation (*actio*). There were of course multiple reasons why Sahlin did not score particularly high in various opinion polls, and why so few people actually understood what she said, but as a rhetoric consultant it was natural for me to look at the rhetorical reasons. And in this case it was her physical actions that came into focus. I looked at how she spoke (the tone) and what she looked like when she spoke (body language). *What* she said became less important because her body language did not harmonize with her message. This does not mean that she didn't actually mean what she said. It means that our interpretation of her tone and body language drowned out the actual message. And then of course there were also those who didn't like the message either.

Your head

If you hold your head slightly to one side you will look critical or vulnerable – depending on your facial expression. The very best is to point your head towards the person you are talking to. If you are pondering a point, or reminiscing, then of course it is natural to look away. It is difficult to keep eye contact when you are away in your dreams. If you want to arouse sympathy and give confirmation when others are talking, nods of your head are very effective. When we talk with people we tend to pay most attention to those who nod. Therefore nodding and listening is a successful combination. If you want to camouflage the fact that you are not listening, nodding can be just as successful, at least for a short time. But if you turn your head away from the person you are talking to, you give the impression of not being interested. Far too many also make the mistake of looking in a different direction – which brings us to eye contact.

Eye contact

In the Bantu language Zulu, the word 'hello' literally means 'I see you'. Make sure you look at the person you meet. When I lectured some of the staff at the Swedish television network SVT in 2005, a woman in the audience felt offended by my very appearance. With her eyes closed, she turned towards me and said, "Elaine, I don't know why I should listen to you who are so young. My spontaneous thought is, what can this snap of a girl teach me?"

She inspired me to write the book *Domination Technique*, so perhaps I should take this chance to thank her. Not looking somebody in the eye often gives an unsympathetic impression. In Western culture it is impolite not to look at the person you are talking to, so the woman with her eyes squeezed shut had the intention of insulting me. There are of course people who don't look at you without having any negative intention. But the consequence of a lack of eye contact is rarely good. If you have taken part in a meeting where everybody – except one person or a couple of people – didn't look at you, you will undoubtedly remember that it was an unpleasant feeling. And you probably don't remember what they said, because your thoughts were busy with the question, 'Why is nobody looking at me?' So if you don't engage in eye contact you're missing the purpose of this book – to get people to listen. (There are, of course, cultural differences, but I am not going to go deeper into those here.)

Since rhetoric is also the art of getting people to listen, it is important that the speaker's voice finds its way into the listener's head and pushes out everything else. An effective way of silencing the listener's inner voice is eye contact. Don't just look at the person who is highest up in the hierarchy when you give a presentation. Look at everybody, as equally as possible! Then you will be regarded as sympathetic and capture the ears of everyone present. Divide the audience into eight sections (if you have a large audience) that you look at in turn. Then everyone will feel that they have been seen. The same applies when you talk to one person. Make sure you have eye contact now and then. Not all the time! If, while speaking to them, you look directly into the eyes of a person you don't know for longer than four seconds, it means 'Shall we kiss and cuddle?' or 'Shall we fight?' If you stare too long, you can make a person embarrassed or angry. The same doesn't apply to the person who is listening. The listener can look for as long as they want. It means nothing more than that they are listening.

Try to control your eyes that little bit extra when you are nervous. They have a tendency to wander from right to left. And talking of right and left, a lot of people ask me which direction you look to when you lie, and when you tell the truth. If I asked you to think of an orange monkey with a purple rosette on its head, you would probably look diagonally up to the left – that is where you construct new images. If, on the other hand, I were to ask you where you travelled to last, you would probably glance diagonally up to the right – that is where your memory centres are situated. This isn't something you need to think about. The listener will in any case not register whether you look to the right or left. But she or he will register that you look away for a third of a second. And that decreases your credibility, especially if it is about an answer that you ought to have close at hand, such as your age. If you ask me how old I am and I look away for a moment before answering '29', you are not going to believe me. At least not as much as you would have if I'd maintained eye contact.

Your mouth

It is a cliché – but it is true – that people who smile often have an easier everyday life for the simple reason that they give an impression of meaning well. It's not difficult to do the math. If you smile, the chances are that you will get smiles back. A lot of people know this, but only a few use it strategically in everyday life.

I decided to do an experiment and marked May 25, 2010, in my calendar. It felt as if the powers above played a trick on me, because on that particular day I woke up with a migraine. But I smiled at my husband before he went off to work. I myself had a three-hour train journey to Karlstad ahead of me. When I got on the train I discovered that I had a seat that meant I would be travelling backwards all the way. But I smiled. I had decided that it would be my new facial expression, regardless of what happened. (Well, for that day at any rate.) When I went to the restaurant carriage I noticed the effect of my chronic smiling. Everybody I met on the way stepped to one side and smiled back. I was given preference because I smiled first. The discovery meant that my smile didn't feel artificial when I reached the restaurant. I smiled with all my face at the woman who worked there. And she smiled back.

"I've got a migraine and I wonder if you sell paracetamol?"

The woman in the bistro picked up her handbag and took out some paracetamol.

"You must have some water too," she said, and fetched a bottle of water from the fridge while I looked for my purse. But she held up her hand and said, "This is on me!" Now my smile was idiotically genuine – and it came with a look of surprise. I was almost worried that I wouldn't be seen as credible at the lecture I was going to give later in the day. On my way back to my seat I swept through the carriages. People smiled and let me pass first. The lecture that I gave just after one of Sweden's most popular speakers, Kjell Enhager, turned out really well. During the entire day I gathered energy as I got back from something I had given – a smile. So my hot tip to you is to test this. Smile for a whole day and see what happens. People in general are more willing to help others who look as though they mean well. Smiles are contagious, just as grumpy looks are. When you have had a bad day, you might know which outside factors and events were the reason. But can you say what you looked like that day?

Body language is important. Let it be in harmony with what you are saying. When I was asked to talk about Swedish Prime Minister Fredrik Reinfeldt's rhetoric, I was shown a film clip where he said, "Time flies when you are having fun!" but his facial expression said something completely different.

Now perhaps you can't entirely blame Reinfeldt. We don't study rhetoric in school here in Sweden, and it is clear which countries do when you see the American president looking happy when he says 'fun'. Not the US, but also England, Australia, Italy and

France have rhetoric as a compulsory subject in school. The art of speaking often goes hand-in-hand with power. Rhetoric ought to be mandatory in school for the sake of democracy. Everyone needs access to the skills it takes to convey a message, but also to see through untruthfulness. And the ability to look at things critically makes it harder for others to gain power over you. (More on this later.) As you think about body language, always make sure your mouth is in harmony with your message. And avoid nervous smiles – if they don't suit the message, that is. If you have something unpleasant to convey, a smile is of course not appropriate.

Your arms

Display open body language, and let your arms be a part of that. It is important that they don't just hang passively to either side of you. Give them a function. There is a myth that says that folded arms are defensive, and intended to shield you. Don't be so sure of that. Lean back where you are sitting and fold your arms in front of you. It's really quite comfortable, isn't it? Most people sit or stand like that for reasons of comfort, so don't over-interpret. But you should look at folded arms in context. If a person folds their arms when you say something nasty, that means they're shielding themselves. Body language should always be seen in the context in which it is observed. But avoid waving your arms too dramatically if you are very close to somebody. Then you are invading their personal space.

Personal space

Some people have no sense of personal space, and that's a sure way to come across as socially incompetent or downright annoying. Adjust your distance from the listener so that you don't intrude upon their buffer of personal space. If the person takes a step back from you, don't follow after! This happens often, and the pursuer can be regarded as pushy. Personal space is relative, depending upon culture and each person's background and disposition. Get a feeling for it so that you don't stand too close, or too far away. (Too far away and the listener will think they smell bad.) If you think that someone is standing too close to you, you can show this in a friendly manner by smiling at the same time that you take a discreet step back. Then the listener will feel properly positioned relative to where you're standing, both physically and mentally. And since you've smiled, the listener will think that you wish them well. You will become aware that you have trespassed on somebody's space if they hold up their hand between the two of you as a defence, or hold up an object like a coffee cup to create even more of a buffer.

When we talk with somebody we often stand half turned away from them, for the simple reason that it is far too intimate to stand directly facing opposite each other. Test this yourself. You will notice that the person you are talking to feels uncomfortable and turns away from you with half their body. Or you will be seen as open to invitations. But it can also mean that you are out to cause trouble. People who are seconds from starting a fight often stand challengingly in front of an adversary, with intensive eye contact. So avoid that sort of stance… unless you want to kiss and cuddle, or fight!

Your hands

Open palms show that you have nothing to hide – an inviting display of body language. Show your palms when you speak, regardless of whether you are having a conversation or making a presentation. It increases your credibility. Open palms also make a conversation feel more easy-going. A person with their hands behind their back, or knitted together, is less credible than a person who opens them towards you now and then.

If you're talking about negative things then you should have your palms facing downwards or raised away from you. Then the listener will see that it is something you are distancing yourself from. Palms facing downwards can be regarded as show of dominance during a conversation. Have them downwards when you talk *about* something negative, not when you talk *to* somebody. Another person can feel dominating if they give you a compliment while putting their hand on your shoulder instead of on your back. To avoid intruding on that person's personal space, the right approach is to give the compliment and open your palm upwards. Hitler, with his stiff-arm salute, displayed a downward palm in the most dominant greeting of all.

Have your palms upwards if you're referencing something you like. Then it will look as if you are offering the listener something. If you want to say stop, then all you have to do is hold up your hands with the palms facing forwards, towards your listeners. (Think of a traffic cop.)

When children lie they hold their hands behind their backs, or together, so that it looks as if they are hiding something. And they avoid eye contact. Some children even put their hands over their mouths. When we grow up we learn to control our gaze, but a lot of people find it difficult to control their hands, for example when they lie or are nervous. It is good to know that our body language when we lie is identical with our body language when we are nervous.

'But what is she up to now?' you might be thinking. 'Is the rhetoric consultant trying to teach us to lie?' Certainly not. You have to decide how to use the information in this book. A good rhetorician should naturally not lie, but those who know the art of rhetoric can sometimes use it to 'smarten up the truth' – we shall see how they do that later on. But back to the similarities between telling lies and being nervous.

Research has shown us that when we lie, or are uptight, the blood vessels in our ears and nose quickly fill. And they start itching. When Bill Clinton said, "I did not have sex with that woman," while scratching his nose, he revealed that he was nervous and (as we now know) almost certainly lied. That lies and nervousness have synonymous expressions means that competent, but nervous, people don't always advance. The reason is simply that they don't give a credible impression.

Avoid using your index finger. An index finger accuses and warns. Hitler used his finger in his speeches, but varied that gesture with a hand on his heart when he spoke about Germany. Sometimes he even raised the palm of his hand to the skies when he talked of the German people. Nobody could misunderstand what he despised and what he honoured deeply. That made him one of the most skilful people of his era when it came to mastering rhetoric. But he was not a *good* rhetorician – it is important to stress that.

What can we learn from this? When an index finger is raised, the person also feels threatened. For example, this gesture might be seen when you are making a presentation and somebody objects to something you've said. There is a great likelihood that your index finger will be raised when you say something like, "What do you mean by that?" The effect can be to deflate the critic because your hand gestures were threatening. If you do feel threatened, don't show it (unless, of course, that is your intended message), but do make an effort to control your hand gestures. After all, you are there to present your message. Show an open palm while you ask, "What do you mean by that?" Then your actions will signal that you are ready to receive criticism. As we've been saying, an open palm is a safe bet.

Avoid having your hands on your face. That arouses suspicion. "I'm telling the truth," said Obama, as he tugged at his ear. Clinton said the same thing and put his hand over his mouth. Don't touch your face or your neck! If something starts to itch while you are saying something, then make sure you mention that so that you don't arouse suspicion.

If somebody puts their hand on their neck while you are speaking to them, then what you are saying is probably making them uncomfortable. Or, at that moment, they are thinking of something uncomfortable. When we are surprised or feel uncomfortable we protect our throats. If we are mortally afraid, then we shield our heads instead. If someone does this when you are talking, perhaps you should change the subject.

In my courses where I teach presentation and rhetoric techniques, I usually make use of the information that body language gives me. (And yes, I realise that my revelation here will make this difficult in future). On the second day I ask everyone in the group to present a three-minute introduction. Earlier, I had asked them to practise running through their remarks seven times, which will total 21 minutes of focused preparation. To gain insight into who has not actually gone through that prep process, I cheerily say, "Welcome to day two! It feels so good to know with complete assurance that every one of you has prepared your presentations." There is no irony in my tone, just an expression of genuine relief. I do this to create a feeling of unease among those who know they're unprepared. When I say that, about one third of the course participants put a hand up to their throats and pull uncomfortably at the skin. These people have not done their homework, and then I know what my expectation level should be for them.

To put them back at ease, I say, "Or perhaps a few of you would like to now spend 21 minutes to prepare and practise?" Then all those hands leave those throats and they wave somewhat guiltily in the air. It is not a big deal. But it is great fun to see how much we communicate with body language.

Your posture and your legs

Straighten your back! It shows self-confidence and provides better support for your voice. Some people want to look relaxed, but you don't have to look like a sack of potatoes to do so. The time will come when you will find it hard to straighten your back. Don't put your body language into early retirement.

Standing with your legs crossed, fiddling with your hair and fidgeting with your fingers are the biggest taboos if you want to look as if you know what you are doing. If you sit with your legs crossed, that of course is not a problem. And remember that you never have to stand frozen behind a podium. It is OK to walk around a little while you talk – if you are giving a presentation, at any rate. And it is nice as well to give your listeners a chance to move their eyes around. That is one of the reasons why, for example, PowerPoint is so anaesthetising. The listener's gaze is fixed on a single place and the buzzing sound from the projector takes us back to the womb. So move around.

When you sit down and have a conversation, your legs should point towards the person you are talking to. That's a sign that you want to engage. One can sense a person's lack of interest, or their unwillingness to talk, by looking at the direction of their legs. If they are pointed towards the door, they've already left you mentally, and will soon want to do so physically. If you yourself want to leave, but want to give the impression of being socially competent, your legs should be pointed towards the person you are talking to. Social competence always trumps domination as a technique, just as being pleasant trumps being overbearing.

If you are in a group of three people talking, then make sure your legs are neutrally oriented, positioned towards the middle. If your legs are pointed just to one person, you are excluding the other. Don't point your legs towards both at the same time; that would just look weird. Keep them in the middle, and nobody is excluded.

If someone sits and has one foot raised – so that it forms a barrier between you and them – you have probably trespassed on their space. If you then lean back when you speak, you will likely signal the listener that you are harmless and he will lower his foot barrier after a while.

We have gone through the body and the importance of body language in getting people to listen, and you have hopefully learnt how to avoid some of the most blatant body language pitfalls. But there are still a few more things to think about.

Shortcuts

If you think that body language is difficult to control at first, try to control one thing: your thoughts. Thoughts steer body language, just as body language steers the dynamics of your voice. And, if you control your thoughts, then your body will follow along. If you think of a high mountain, I promise you that you will look up and have the palms of your hands upwards when you say, "It was an enormous mountain." The same applies if you think about something small. You will look down, lower your shoulders and show the small distance between your thumb and index finger while you say, "It was really tiny." We think in images. If you concentrate on what you say you will also visualise it and with body language articulate what you see. So silence that nervous inner voice that whispers, 'This is a horrible situation'. Otherwise your body language will signal that you're really scared, while you say aloud, "How nice to see you!"

By all means study good conversationalists, professional hosts and masters of ceremonies. Watch how they behave and learn from it. A lot of people ask me who I consider the best rhetorician. My answer is always, "The person who catches the listener's attention and convinces them." Who that is, and how it is done, is relative. There are many ways. Try to find what suits your workplace, or those situations where you're going to step up and be the best communicator in the room.

5 How to get your message to sink in

Far too many people think that to get their message to sink in, they only have to verbalize it. Unfortunately, that is not the case; if it were so simple then there would be no need for us rhetoric consultants. I have had a number of clients who have been exasperated over the fact that the company's motto is one thing but how their customers describe them is quite another. "We have even written our motto on our home page!" they say, failing to understand. They may have posted their message on the web, but that doesn't mean it's made any sort of impression on their customers. For somebody to understand that you are in love with him or her, it is not enough to simply say it. It is of course very satisfying to hear that one's feelings are reciprocated, but other components come into play – such as body language, the tone of your voice, the mood and your actions – to really *convince you* that the person is in love with you.

In order to get people to absorb your message as quickly as possible, you have to put yourself in their shoes and ask three questions.

The first question to imagine your listener mulling over is, 'Who are you?' Even if it is your first meeting, other people will come to various conclusions about you extremely quickly. Try to create an atmosphere around you that is comfortable and pleasant. And combine that with credibility relative to what you are going to talk about. Don't say your name for the first few seconds. Nobody is going to register that. Gradually the listener is going to wonder why you don't introduce yourself, and they will remember your name after you eventually do. The exception, of course, is when you greet somebody for the first time with a handshake. Then it is of course customary to exchange names right away. The messenger is always as important as the message, and we quickly decide if we are going to like a person or not. And whether that person is credible.

A rhetoric consultant, for example, ought to say that she has an academic foundation, just as you shouldn't call yourself an economist without having studied the subject. Combine the 'nice person' vibe with an underlying sense of credibility, and then say your name. The listener will then remember it.

The second question you must imagine your listener asking is, 'What are you going to talk about?' Say this quickly and efficiently and then expand upon it in the answer to the third question.

And that final question you must imaging your listener asking is, 'What's in it for me?' In the long run that is really the foremost question. That is the nagging, subconscious question the listener has while you are talking. How will the listener benefit from hearing your message? What's important is not how you, who are communicating the message, will benefit – unless the listener is for some reason interested in that. Don't over-embroider your answer, so that it overshadows the listener's benefit.

If I want to persuade my husband that we should travel to Brazil for the fourth year in a row, the big, motivating driver can't be, 'Because I want to'. Rather, I must present the idea so that he realises how he will benefit from a journey to Brazil. So, how do you translate your message into an answer to the 'what is the benefit for the listener' question? You have come a long way already by just asking that question; far too many people are preoccupied with just sending the message. When it comes to my husband, I use a method that you will find in the chapter 'The Art of Persuasion – the Technique of Argumentation'. And yes, we will be travelling to Brazil once again this year.

Far too many salesmen, and communicators in general, go on about 'objective truths' as to whether something is 'good'. But, for the consumer, whether something is good is only relevant if it is good for them. So, it isn't sufficient to claim that something is good. That doesn't affect people in at all the same way as when the message is tailored, customized, adapted. You will certainly have met people, socially as well as professionally, who babble on without a thought as to whether what they are saying is of any interest to you. They don't ask any questions. Nor do they even pretend to be interested in what you may think. When they do finally ask a question it is usually phrased in such a way as to give them an excuse to continue to babble even more. "Have you been in Boa Vista in northern Brazil? No? I didn't think you had, but I have and..." These monologue monsters only talk about things they themselves find interesting. The consequence is that you eventually lose interest. Don't make the same mistake. Skilful salesmen succeed in asking questions that give them information about the buyer. They listen carefully and get the buyer to feel that they have been seen and are valuable. And, of course, the buyer is valuable. But we mustn't forget that the information we get from them is also valuable. Take, for example, someone who is shopping for a telephone. Imagine that they don't want the latest smart phone, but simply a phone that you can make a call with. Unfortunately, the salesman is determined to run through every brilliant argument for getting an iPhone.

"Here's an iPhone, and just look how simple it is!"

"But it hasn't got any press buttons."

"Oh yes it has, but these are much simpler buttons that can't fall off or break. Just look," says the salesman as he draws his finger across the screen.

"But all these symbols – what are they? I only want to phone people."

"And that is exactly what's so nice about the iPhone. You *can* just ring people with it whenever you want," says the salesman as he deletes the apps. "It's just so simple!"

The salesman doesn't say the same thing when a tech-savvy customer comes along. But he's selling the same product. Now he doesn't say that the telephone is best, but that it is best *for you*. And that is the point. Even though the message is the same, it shouldn't be understood to be so by everyone. Think about how you can formulate the message so that the answer to 'What's in it for me?' is relevant and interesting for the listener. Make the message attractive to the listener.

Feelings to arouse

In order to increase listener motivation to the maximum, you should arouse three feelings. Some of the feelings can be baked into the three questions that you should answer, but sometimes you need to be more creative. The three feelings that you need to create are goodwill, credibility and curiosity. Unfortunately, when we don't like a person our listener motivation drops to zero. It doesn't make any difference how good the message is, if I don't like you then I am not going to listen. So in every given situation, you need to think about how you can get people to like you. It can be anything from looking them in the eye and smiling when you introduce yourself, to taking a bowl of sweets to the staff meeting. Small things really can make a big difference in generating goodwill and pulling people into your rhetorical grasp. Credibility is important – you need to give them reason to think that you know what you are talking about. There are different ways of demonstrating credibility. A hobby rhetorician began a presentation on rhetoric with the words, "I am not an academic rhetoric consultant, but I am bloody good at talking and now you will find out why." She aroused goodwill with her plainspoken confession, and sparked interest and credibility with those last two phrases. Coach Mia Törnblom is no 'brain researcher', she usually confesses, nor does she have any certificates or diplomas. "I might not have academic qualifications, but I climbed out of the swamp of drugs," she says, "and I can teach you how to get out of difficult situations." She confesses, and she becomes more credible thanks to that. Think about how you might seem more credible to the people you are going to communicate with.

Structure your message

I often say that there are three types of audiences. There are those who absolutely love to listen to the experiences of others. Then there are those who think that hard facts, statistics and scientific investigations are the most exciting form of information. And the third category wants to hear emotional stories of all types, just as long as they arouse feelings. To get all categories to want to listen to you, you should have included three components in your message: experience, facts and feelings. The rhetorical translations for these words are *ethos* (experience), *logos* (facts) and *pathos* (feeling).

But you also want your listeners to remember what you have said. Sometimes you can leave a meeting with the feeling that it has gone well, but you can't describe it properly. There are special stylistic devices, such as rhetorical figures that are a regular pattern in speech, or text, and that help you to get others to remember what you have said. They can be various types of repetition of words, or the use of an apostrophe, exclamations or rhetorical questions. Lennart Hellspong, a professor of Rhetoric, has asserted that stylistic devices help to arouse attention, create understanding, win approval and prompt a reaction.

Stylistic devices (figures of speech)

Rhetorical figures are effective aids to get the listener to remember what you have said. They are made so that they become formulations that are easy to remember. It can even be difficult to try to forget them once you have started using them. They beat every PowerPoint presentation in the world, because with PowerPoint you get the message on a screen. But with a stylistic device you get the message in your brain, which makes it that much sharper.

For example, I wanted my rhetorical agency to stick out and have a name that everybody would remember. The stylistic device of alliteration did the job. The result was the Swedish phrase *Snacka Snyggt* (literally 'Talk Nicely', but perhaps 'Chat Charmingly' would be a better equivalent). Alliteration is when words that are close to each other have rhyming letters – they start with the same letter, or the same sound, for example. *Snacka Snyggt* is easy to remember; the alliteration makes it hard to forget.

Paraphrasing is good when you want to drive home a message. That means saying the same thing but in different ways: 'Rhetoric is the art of getting people to listen', 'Rhetoric is the art of getting people to pay attention', 'Rhetoric is the art of getting people to want to hear more'. Try to think up various ways of presenting your message so that the point really does land with the listener. This method is often used in media training. We see the result especially when politicians are interviewed on TV. The person gets a question and answers by saying the same thing, but in different ways.

Anaphora (a Greek word which literally means 'carrying back') is when a series of sentences begin with the same words or phrases. The use of anaphora characterized the most effective part of Martin Luther King's *I Have a Dream* speech. Use anaphora so that your listeners will remember. But there is also a risk. A classic Swedish example is the responses by government minister Bosse Ringholm at a press conference in 1999. Ringholm provided precisely the same answer to all the questions throughout the conference: "She has expressed interest in another task." But repetition isn't good if you get different questions. Instead of paraphrasing, which is providing variations of the same answer, he went for an anaphora: identical answers repeated many times. If a journalist had asked "Can you dance the salsa?" Ringholm would have presumably answered with the same anaphora.

During the general election in 2010, party leader Lars Ohly used *circumlocution*. Circumlocution is when you use another word for a well-known and ordinary concept, based on its content. Ohly called the Left Party 'The Welfare Party', since that was a quality of the Left Party that he wanted people to focus upon and associate with the party.

Allusion (which has its origin in the Latin verb *ludere* meaning 'to play with, to jest') is a common strategy in fiction. Within rhetoric you can use it to arouse attention. You can, for example, refer to a well-known quote and replace it with your own words. "I have a dream," said Martin Luther King with his hand raised. "I have a mate!" you can say repeatedly, with your hand raised in your next toast at a wedding dinner.

Climax (from the Greek *Klimax*, literally meaning a staircase or ladder) is leveraged when you want to increase the intensity in a speech. It is a figure of speech where the parts are arranged in order of increasing importance. A series of parts with growing intensity in your voice, body language and message. If you want to heat up an anaphora with climax, you only need to raise your voice more and more for each sentence. Test it yourself! "I like this book. I like this book! I like this book!!!" (Repeat that sentence in the nearest public place!)

Metaphor is an expression in imagery. This is the rhetorical figure where an item and a concept are changed for something else that is equivalent, and then describing that part with an image. "We shall get the company's engine going again", you might say when you are really referring to the economy. Imagery is extremely effective since we think in images. And yes, when you talk you can control the images you want people to visualise mentally.

Anthropomorphism is when we give an object human qualities and intentions. 'The snow is driving us crazy', 'The darkness is threatening us.'

Similes are effective if you want to associate a certain person, or subject, with a certain feeling. 'He's as crafty as a snake' is a simile that arouses negative associations. You can steer your similes so that they conjure what you intend, depending on which feelings you want to arouse in your listener – positive or negative, inspiring or sad? There are lots of choices.

Allegory is a smart stylistic figure if you want to talk about something discreetly. An allegory conveys hidden meaning. You say and describe something other than that which is concretely presented. The indirect means of expression leaves things open to interpretation and thus frees you from responsibility. You can always claim that it is a matter of interpretation. George Orwell's novel *Animal Farm* was an allegory, where the animals represented communism without him ever directly naming that political system.

Paradox is when you place opposites together in the same sentence, or in a context. "To think that something so little can produce something so large," a friend of mine exclaimed when she had just become a mother and stood there changing a nappy. A paradox can have quite an effect, even though the paradox is not expressly stated. It could, for example, be that the expectation you have of what a repairman looks like can be quite unlike the actual appearance of the man who arrives at your front door.

Remember that stylistic figures should sound natural. A lot of people come with a pile of them that are so formal and forced you would think they urgently needed to go the loo. Or they articulate the stylistic figures with exaggerated clarity; they become the stereotype of a rhetorician, standing there, rigid, t-a-l-k-i-n-g s-l-o-w-l-y. You will no doubt have heard politicians whose speechwriters are keen on stylistic figures. Unfortunately, the speech doesn't come off sounding particularly personal, even though the candidate is arguing that he will fairly represent you. Make the stylistic figure your own so that you can say it in a relaxed way. Then it will sound natural for the listener. In other words, relax and let your rhetoric flow.

Create a mental rhetorical place

And so, we have travelled part of the way on your journey of rhetorical development. The next step is for you to find a place where you can be the best rhetorical version of yourself. Going forward, you'll have this special place with you regardless of the rhetorical challenge.

I want you to think of a miss in communication that you made in the past. It can be anything from when you babbled on while those around you were not interested, to your being silent when the listeners waited for what you were going to say. Then I want you to think of a situation where everyone listened to you. As I mentioned in the introduction, it could be when you sat in a garden, talking to a good friend. Or when you gave a presentation at work that went better than expected. When you think back on a real-life miss and a genuine success, you have a rhetorical scale for when you were a bad rhetorical version of yourself and when you were the best. Let's think about the good outcome and develop that.

To make sure that your rhetorical place is accessible it is good for it to be as tangible a place as possible. It could be your grandmother's armchair, a bar with a best friend or perhaps those conversations with you partner at home on your sofa.

A course participant I was training was really nervous when she had to give a presentation on day two. It was a nervousness that bordered on fear. Before she started her presentation, I talked with her in a way that would get her to forget the speaker-audience dynamic and get in a state of mind where she felt calm.

"Annelie, what was your mental place?"

"Our armchairs in the living room."

So that she could more effectively move to her mental place, I asked her to describe the living room and what the armchairs looked like.

"The armchairs are white, the wallpaper flowery, and we have a little fireplace too."

"Who do you usually sit with?"

Annelie's face lit up and she said, "My daughter." She had left her speaker situation and was now in her mental place. That is an effective way to handle nervousness. Annelie's rhetoric was like how she'd naturally talk with someone when she was relaxed and comfortable. Now, all she had to do was start the presentation.

When you find yourself in situations where you think it is an extra challenge to communicate successfully, I want you to think back to that time when you did exceptionally well. Regardless of whether the place where that happened is a garden or a bar, it should always be with you. When you are in a job interview, or negotiating a pay raise, or perhaps when you have to give somebody criticism, think that you are there – in your mental place – and your rhetoric is likely to be discernibly better.

As I mentioned earlier, there is a surfeit of professional robots in Sweden. They could benefit greatly from a mental rhetorical place. That salesperson with her clichés ought to think that she's selling to a friend instead. The bank official ought to give financial advice as if he was giving it to his daughter. The shop assistant would do well to imagine answering questions from his mother.

A good friend of mine was going to buy a telephone, a Nokia, many years ago. He went from one phone shop to the next, and he left them as quickly as he entered because of pushy salespeople. "They were probably yellow people," he claimed. They were their professional selves, too. In the end he came to shop where the salespeople were content with just welcoming him and then letting him look around on his own. "That was the breathing space I need to want to buy anything at all," he said. Finally he called one of the salespeople, who was named Peter, over to him. My friend asked to look at the Nokia and Peter gave him a down-to-earth explanation of its advantages. Then my friend leaned closer and asked with a sceptical expression, "But Peter, what do you really think?" The young man was rather taken aback by this, took a deep breath, looked around, and then looked back at my friend. He whispered, "Don't tell my boss, but this telephone sucks. Let me show you another one." My friend felt giggly and ready to make a purchase because now he wasn't buying from some random salesperson but from Peter, who happened to be a salesperson. It might have been a sales trick, but it works so much better when people dare to be themselves. What struck my friend was that Peter managed to be himself in his professional environment. Perhaps he had his own mental rhetorical place, which made such a thing possible.

Professor Hans Rosling, whom I mentioned earlier, is the same rhetorically when he stands on a stage in front of 2,000 people and when he is at home, seated at the kitchen table with four members of his family. Perhaps his mental rhetorical place is precisely that family dinner, and perhaps that helps explain why he has become Sweden's most successful lecturer.

I have quite a lively temperament, and I have a mental place that helps me keep my temper in check when I come across bully types. It doesn't always work, but it often does. I think about my one-year-old, Matheo, visualise his face, and then it is much harder for me to get angry.

Your thoughts affect feelings in your body, which is why angry thoughts make your heart beat faster and happy thoughts bring feelings of joy. Make sure you have the right thoughts at hand when you want to convey a rhetorical message that is beneficial to you.

In other words, you can have different mental places depending on what sort of person you're dealing with and what you want to achieve through communicating with them. If you know that you tend to babble on at times, you can rein yourself in by creating a mental place that necessitates being silent – perhaps a church. If your temper is hard to control, think about somebody or something that makes you happy and harmonious. If you have stage fright when you are going to talk in front of a large group, your mental place is more important than ever. You should not 'imagine that your audience is naked', as is often suggested, but visualise that place where you feel 100% safe. Then you can imagine that the people sitting in the audience are those who are closest to your heart and talk in the way you would have talked to them.

You can also make use of physical places – such as where you position yourself at the table or on a stage – to hold your audience's attention. That can be effective when you give presentations. If you look at your content, you'll find that you'll perhaps be delivering varying messages, ranging from downbeat to pleasant. To make it easier for listeners to follow along with you on your rhetorical journey, you can literally change places when you switch from talking about the dreary things to talking about the more uplifting things. It is about doing something as little as taking one step to the left. I had a course participant who did this superbly. He said he was going to say something that was true and something that was false. In providing this setup, when he said 'true' he pointed to the right side of his body, and he motioned to the left side when he said 'false'. Then, when he started talking about that which was true, he took a step to his right, and when he went on to talk about what was false he took a step to his left. It was a very simple but effective way to follow along with his message.

When you sit and talk with somebody, you don't have to get up and move around, but can help show what you mean with your hands. You will certainly have met people who instinctively use *the place method* when they converse. They can talk about something invisible that they appear to actually look at and show on the table. That might seem meaningless, but it is in fact important because the listener can follow along more easily. I can point to a place you showed on the table and say, "But is that figure really correct?" even though the figure isn't there at all. But it is there mentally, for both of us.

You can also quite simply look a little to the right, left, up or down when you talk about different things. It was such fun to hear my friend Catherine talk about her four colleagues. She looked to the right when she described one of them, down and waving towards the table when she described one she didn't like, higher up about another colleague and upwards when she described her boss. I thought it was weird when she looked up when she talked about her boss so I asked her if her workplace was hierarchical. She was slightly confounded and asked how I knew?

The direction in which you look when you use mental places doesn't really matter, but remember that upwards and downwards can be interpreted as your looking up to, or down at, the person or thing you are talking about.

Chapter

1

How to get people to like you in three minutes

The year was 2002 and the day was The Big Rhetoric Day that we rhetoric students had arranged. The hall was full and we had managed to book established lecturers. We had particularly high hopes for one of them. She was a popular lecturer with a good reputation. But that day something strange happened. She walked with heavy steps up to the microphone on stage. She looked tired and uninvolved, as if she didn't want to be there. Everybody waited. After a long sigh she said, "I slept really badly last night and I don't really have the energy to be here... but I shall do my best."

The audience gasped. Was this a joke? No, it wasn't. The time it took for her to say those words was also totally wasted – for her as well as us. It is important that the person who is speaking arouses goodwill if the message is to land softly (or land at all). The valuable time should feel worth its price. We had given other things a lower priority so that we could listen to her. I remember that I thought that I didn't like her. It didn't matter how much she ran around on the stage and tried to capture our attention after that dreadful start. We had already dismissed her. The first impression sticks – for a long time. There are people who got off to a bad start in a working relationship, and never ended up getting on properly with that colleague. The very beginning is in many ways decisive; there are psychological explanations as to why. Judging a person based on a single quality is called the halo effect. The *halo effect* is a specific form of the general representativity effect (which I mentioned when we talked about strategic dressing choices earlier in the book). It means that a person who gives a good impression – and who we think looks nice – is also regarded as kind, generous and good in other ways. The first impression overshadows or embellishes the later ones, and vice versa. If you are not nice, the listener will draw other negative conclusions about you and your presentation. This woman started negatively and that meant that we, the audience, charged the rest of the lecture with critical judgements.

The lecture lasted one hour. It is interesting to note that one student colleague who came ten minutes late had a totally different appraisal. This colleague sat on the edge of her seat and listened with all her senses. And applauded. She didn't seem to notice that the rest of us sat with our arms folded to demonstrate our dissatisfaction. Students who arrived late thought that it was one of the best lectures they had heard. We others thought it was one of the worst. How could that be? Well, we had experienced totally different introductions (*exordium*) and thus the halo effects were different too. The others missed the bad start. They saw her through another 'filter'. This filter is created while the listener decides what sort of person they're dealing with. And that happens in the first three minutes.

On one occasion, an established lecturer started by saying: "Now the lecture has only gone on for one minute and I have already earned 10,000 kronor." He followed this with a short laugh. But nobody in the audience laughed. After all, it wasn't his own personal profit he was meant to be lecturing about. Afterwards, there was massive criticism. And despite the fact that he was well known (with his own TV programme) he wasn't allowed to lecture on the additional days he had been booked for. Being a celebrity does not mean you are an exception from the three-minute rule. You can't just rely on a good old reputation. You must maintain it, too.

Credibility, goodwill, curiosity

Regardless of the context and your celebrity status, you have three minutes to create a filter through which your listener will observe you. These three minutes are crucial for the rest of the conversation, presentation or meeting. That is when the listener decides whether they experience you as sympathetic and credible. And if what you are talking about is relevant. So it is crucial that during those three minutes you arouse three feelings: 1. *docilis*, make the listener ready to learn by making the subject relevant for them; 2. *benevelus*, arouse goodwill; 3. *attentus*, make the listener attentive. Putting it simply, you have three minutes to create:

- Credibility
- Goodwill
- Curiosity

So how do you succeed in doing that? Imagine that you've created the opposite – ill will, distrust and irrelevance. It's easier than you'd think for things to slide in the wrong direction.

Credibility

In the first few seconds of meeting someone, your handshake can literally make or break your credibility. Do you want a meeting to fail? Use the 'dead fish', where a person's hand lands in yours and it feels like… well, you get the picture. You squeeze it in a friendly manner but don't get any response. The fingers of the other person sort of squash together inside your hand and this gives you an inexplicable feeling that you don't like them at all. The handshake lets you know that this is a passive and indifferent person, and likely as exciting as watching paint drying. Despite the fact that you have only just met, this person has involuntarily given you a filter through which you will observe them for the rest of the meeting. And it is not an attractive filter.

The handshake is extremely important. It is when you literally have a chance to press in your credibility. The pressure in a handshake is, of course, relative, but the key is to meet the listener's strength. You can read a lot in a handshake, and the aim is for the listener to read you in a way that is to your advantage. So, it is important that you give a handshake that inspires confidence.

The dominator

When shaking hands, a dominant person often puts their hand over yours. He or she can give a slight twist when you have grasped each other's hands so that yours ends up underneath. If you want to hold your ground against the dominator, you should smile and twist your hands back so that they're both once again vertical. That sends a signal that they can't overpower you.

The robot

The robot handshake wants to compete in strength and send the signal, 'I can crush you here and now'. The person takes hold of your hand and presses unnecessarily hard. This is the sort of person who feels that they have a lot to prove. Personally, I don't try to match them in competition. It feels as if it is more about testosterone levels than anything else. The robot handshake is a really silly one that you should steer clear of. Like the dead fish, the robot should never be used – ever.

The pincher

The pincher handshake is when the person only pinches your fingers. Stressed people often do this, and is not a path to goodwill. Avoid pinching fingertips.

A lot of people often make the mistake, when there is a large crowd, of looking over to the next person they are going to greet while still holding somebody else's hand. It gives an unsympathetic impression and makes the person who was looked away from feel unimportant. On the other hand, it is not rare for those with power to have the ability to make people they meet feel *chosen*. That is why many people with newly acquired recognition and authority think that they can act like a diva, which causes others to lose respect for them. And, in losing respect, they lost power. If you don't see others, they stop seeing you. After the handshake, during the meeting, you should of course pull out other reasons to prove your credibility. But, during those first few seconds, reliability is often embodied in three things: accomplishing a good handshake; establishing eye contact;

remembering the person's name. If you fumble through a bad handshake, you only have to say, "Can we do that again?" and press forward with a nice, new grasp. That will certainly give the other person a better grasp of your credibility. To arouse goodwill, meet the other person's strength in the handshake and look them in the eye.

You should avoid certain words that might arouse distrust. And avoid repeating words too often. When Barack Obama became President, his rhetorical ticks crept out. Obama has been criticized for using arcane, professorial terminology and not always being clear. After the criticism reached the White House he began to often say, "Now, let me be clear," while simultaneously raising his index finger. That particular sentence arouses distrust since you then can easily start wondering whether he is not clear on other occasions. An amusing observation is that as soon as Obama says, "Let me be clear," it's generally followed by something that is completely unintelligible. Just like the double-talk that can result when people don't want to answer a question. Then they praise the formulation by saying, "That was an excellent question." The questioner is satisfied for the time being, and doesn't notice until later that he/she doesn't get an answer. Giving a non-answer is one way to slowly but surely decrease one's credibility.

There are several terminological pitfalls you ought to avoid:

- 'In actual fact' – The implication is that nothing else you say is factual
- 'Well, to be honest' – Then people will wonder if you usually lie
- 'Just a few words about' – Apologetic rhetoric cause the listener to lose interest
- Arcane concepts and abbreviations – Use words that everybody understands.
- 'I have a *small* question' – Don't qualify your words; just say, 'I have a question'. Let the listener deal with that judgement

In the book *Trovärdighet – så bigger du förtroende* (Credibility – how to build confidence), rhetoric consultant Katti Sandberg writes, 'Credibility is a necessity to achieve successful communication, while at the same time credibility is a result of successful communication.' To be credible, your choice of words and the picture of you and what you say must feel credible. Don't misunderstand me. To be credible does not mean that you as an engineer should use an engineer's terminology; the listener would understand that you're smart, but not have a clue what you're talking about. The listener wants to understand everything you say. If they don't, they will feel stupid. That is why I don't understand rhetoricians who talk a language that nobody understands. Besides, 'communication' comes from the Latin verb *communicare*, meaning to share. Don't isolate yourself on an island of words that only you understand. Don't make yourself look brainy – make yourself understood!

In body language, credibility sits in your eyes and hands. You certainly will have been in meetings where some people never look *at* you. You don't remember what they said, but you do remember that they did *not* look at you. And that arouses distrust. So look at the people you are talking with, if in a group. Otherwise, look at the person you are talking with *in the eye*. But not, as I pointed out earlier, all the time. It is natural to look away when you are thinking about something, weighing up things, imagining something. That is perfectly alright. The listener won't lose focus since what you are doing will be reflected in your body language. We have mentioned the palms of your hands, and when it comes to credibility these are particularly important. If you're having a coffee and snack with a friend who sits with their hands behind their back throughout the conversation, it would feel wrong. We show our palms when we speak – subconsciously. You can steer this best by directing your thoughts towards what you are talking about; your body language will follow along.

Remember, too, not to look at your watch (or a wall clock, or your smartphone). The other person will feel smaller when you convey that you have something more important to think about.

Goodwill

Combine the handshake and eye contact with a smile and that will make for a good start. I know a lot of people with the perfect hand-shake, but with a facial expression that looks like they have just been to a funeral. The message then becomes that this person is not happy to see you. A simple rule is to always smile – unless the purpose of the meeting is to say something really, *really* unpleasant. Some people even smile in that situation, so that the listener will think, 'The news is unpleasant, but at least I like the presenter of that news'. You do not need to personify your message before you convey it. If you are happy, it will show, and your choice of words will be positive too. If it feels difficult to glue on a smile, you can think about a special place, or person who puts you in a good mood. Then your body language will look genuinely happy. I mentioned earlier, in the section on body language, that a short-cut to effectively steering your body language is to visualize what you are talking about. Or envision a person or place you like. Have that mental picture with you when you greet people, especially if you are nervous. It can even be good when you greet somebody you don't like, since your smile can change the relationship.

Nicholas Boothman, photographer and author of the relation-ship book *How to Make People Like You in 90 Seconds or Less* thinks that you can trigger a positive memory by, for example, having a special movement associated with that memory. Perhaps you think repeatedly about that summer evening with your best friend, while simultaneously squeezing your thumb with your hand. Gradually your brain will learn to associate the thumb with that summer memory. That means you will have a positive mem-ory at hand when you meet others, you will project a genuinely positive impression, and they will pick up on it.

Curiosity

I think back to a day when I was attending Södertorn University in Stockholm. My fellow student and present rhetoric colleague Jennie Gotsis and I were going to have our first rhetoric seminar for a group of students who studied Swedish. We were both rather nervous. We decided that Jennie should greet each one of them at the entrance with a handshake. I would prepare the films we were going to show. Seventy students dropped in, one after the other. I thought that shaking hands with all of them was overkill but Jennie thought otherwise. She had a bit of a glazed look about her every time one of the students said their name. And she didn't let go until she had heard the name properly. She even held her grip when they were silent. I thought that seemed uncomfortably long, even though it was only a matter of a second or two. When the entire group had settled in their seats, one of them put up her hand.

"Yes, Malin?" Jennie asked the brunette who put up her hand. Malin was speechless. I was speechless. Malin didn't have a name label. But Jennie still knew her name. 'Luck!' was my spontaneous thought and I felt safe again.

"Why did you greet each of us at the beginning?" asked Malin. "That has never happened before. I thought it was good, but I wonder why you did it."

"In rhetoric, credibility and goodwill are two of three elements that you need to arouse in new listeners. I wanted my greeting to arouse credibility and goodwill," Jennie answered.

"I think you aroused goodwill, but where does the credibility come in?" asked a guy sitting in the back.

"Good question, Fredrik," answered Jennie. "By memorising all your names."

Another participant turned his attention towards me. "And you, Elaine – do you remember all our names too?" I felt a bit pressed, and answered:

"Unfortunately, Michael (of course that wasn't his name), unlike Jennie here, I am just an ordinary human being."

Everyone laughed at my flimsy, light hearted excuse. Credibility, goodwill and curiosity were now in place. We could start the seminar.

When former US Vice President and presidential candidate Al Gore was in Sweden some years ago, he had a brief exchange with a journalist. When the same journalist met Gore five years later, the politician addressed him by his name. Without great effort and using simple memory technique, Gore had placed himself on a high level of respect. Nelson Mandela too, when he was active, was careful to memorize names. Not only of those who liked him, but also those who disliked him. The fact that he remembered the names of the apartheid supporters meant that they, albeit unwillingly, felt a certain degree of goodwill and respect for him. He knew he needed to win over his opponents, not just those who already supported his cause.

Most people in high positions have polished rhetoric, but often a good memory too. If they don't, they have an assistant who notes all names and gives them a quick briefing before a meeting, as did Al Gore. Everything to give the journalist a good impression and create goodwill. To get to the top you need a large network of people. Remembering names is the road there. A lot of skilled leaders know that and are therefore rather manic about the ability to remember names. What you are saying, between the lines, to the person whose name you remember is, 'You are worth remembering, you mean something, you are an important person.' And the karma effect becomes that he or she will think the same about you. Henrik Fexeus writes in his book *The Art of Reading Minds*, 'We like people when they say that they like us.' When you remember names, you arouse just such a feeling. So how is it done?

The first obstacle when it comes to memory technique is our inner voice. When we meet a new person, it echoes automatically inside our heads. We want to figure out what we think about them. See if he or she belongs to the same flock, is like us, and so on. That is why you must turn off that inner voice so that this person actually reaches you and can be heard and thus leave an impression – their name. Turn off, and concentrate on what the person says. If she is called, for example, Estelle, you can create a crazy picture inside your head of her nostrils shouting out Estelle. Absurd? Yes, but that's the sort of thing we remember. Create several pictures inside your head. She perhaps screams 'Estelle', or the liver spot on her chin can change to an E. Connect memory pictures with things that can't change on Estelle. Her hairstyle is perhaps not a good idea. But think of her mouth, eyes, nose or other details that tend to be permanent. Don't have enough imagination? Then say, "Hello Estelle!" when she says her name, press her hand and smile while you repeat it.

The useless excuse, 'I must concentrate on saying my own name, that is why I can't remember other people's names' is not good enough. We have had our names since we were born. You are not going to say 'I am Underpants' just because you are not concentrating on your name. Relax. Focus on the other person's name. Yours will come by itself.

On certain occasions, we are also especially good at concentrating. For some strange reason our concentration becomes greater when we ask children what they are called. And we often remember their names. Apply that same attention when you meet adults. So, when the person you are greeting says her name is Alice, answer, "Alice. Nice to meet you Alice, I'm Elaine." Or quite simply: "Alice. Nice, Alice... Elaine!" Then you have repeated their name once, used it once more, and introduced your own name into the mix as well. If you succeed, you won't just have made a good impression but they'll remember you for the simple reason that you remembered their name.

Mirroring body language - rapport

When you establish rapport you achieve a certain flow in the conversation and establish a good relationship. It is good to mirror the other person's body language. If the person talks about something sad, it is a good idea if you look like them. Then they will feel that you really are with them and understand what they are saying.

A lack of flow (or anti-rapport, one might call it) is if you smile when somebody says something sad, or if you take a step towards your conversation partner and insist on talking at kissing distance (that is what it feels like) even though they step back. Adapt to the person you are talking to. Don't put any value on physical closeness, but mark what you yourself want and accept that the distance looks like it should be further. We Swedes are not always regarded as people who keep their distance; in some cultures we are seen as forward. Everything is relative.

So goodwill is a combination of a good handshake, memory technique and rapport in body language, voice and mood. Make sure you utilise these. Then you will be experienced as memorable and nice. And your meetings will be successful. This makes a big difference… at first, anyway.

Three minutes

A good start doesn't take long, and it leads to long-term good relations – both professional and personal. It doesn't matter if somebody else in the context is unsympathetic. Make an effort; it is an investment that will pay off. If you have decided to win the start, then the person who has not been pleasant will gradually get a bad conscience. Don't make the same mistake that many others do in the first few minutes, those who scan the person they meet for the first time to decide what attitude they should have toward her or him. There's always this to consider: the other person is scanning you at the same time. Have that in focus instead and make sure you make a good impression. Then their radar will pick up 'goodwill', 'curiosity' and 'credibility' as quickly as possible.

Companies, too, should be better at *the first three minutes* and invest in the environment an employee first meets a customer when he or she steps into the building. Make sure it feels inviting, safe and inspires confidence. I have studied waiting rooms at many companies and been amazed at the variation. Some simply splash out money. Others make a considerable effort to make you feel comfortable – and, in a sense, earn money in that way.

When I visited a clinic recently, the environment impressed me. When I came to the reception area, the woman behind the counter saw me, even though she was talking with another patient. She smiled, greeted me and pointed to the sofas. They were a virginal white – brilliant! On the walls they had TV screens with pictures of bodies labelled with rhetorical questions such as, 'What do you want to change?' What is so smart about rhetorical questions is that they make the listener think along the paths that the questions direct. Before the TV commercials asked us, 'Do you too suffer from split ends?' none of us knew that we suffered from split ends. The commercials led us along those paths and got us to buy the supposed solution. I sat in the white sofa and looked at the screens. Before-and-after pictures. I put my hands on my stomach. Thought about whether I had wrinkles too. Slowly but surely, this clinic became the salvation from the frightening rhetoric they had planted in the waiting room. I had accepted their argument since their receptionist and environment had aroused goodwill and credibility, their TV screens curiosity. But, what is so delightful about rhetoric is that you can learn to see through it. So there was no plastic surgery for me, even though the environment increased the likelihood.

When you enter a business, it is the entrance area that creates the first impression. One of my customers let me wait ten minutes, and during that time I could enjoy their boastful, but skilfully furnished, waiting room. I had a nice cup of coffee and a lovely view! What does the reception area look like at your job?

See yourself as a 'reception' in the meeting with new people, and make sure that they leave with a good impression. It takes at most three minutes to plant a good impression. Invest in those precious minutes. And remember that those three first minutes will be about:

1. Your handshake
2. Your smile
3. Remembering the person's name
4. Establishing eye contact
5. Letting your palms be open when you talk
6. Creating rapport when the person talks
7. Respecting the listener's personal space

If you want the effect to last a long time, don't forget to carry the feeling that the first impression created through to future meetings. Goodwill, curiosity and credibility are not just something you should arouse, but also maintain.

So, you have managed your introduction. It is now time to think about how you will get the conversation to roll smoothly. It is basically about getting others to want to listen to you, and paradoxically it is listening that can be the road there.

Chapter

Conversation
technique

A bore talks only about himself, a gossip only about others. But a skilled conversationalist talks about you – with you. He will get you hooked from the very first. You've certainly tried to talk with somebody who only gives yes or no answers.

Perhaps you have met a monologue monster, one of those people who don't let anyone else get a word in edgeways. If you try to say something, they smile, raise their voice and continue. They cut you off, draw parallels to themselves and fill in sentences you have begun. They have not mastered the art of listening. They break all the conversation taboos there are, and the 'conversation' is either very short, or murderously long. If you like talking, there is a risk that you yourself may be a monologue monster. Or perhaps you might have problems taking your share, or finding exciting subjects to talk about.

When it comes to conversation technique, it is actually the introvert who is better off than the extrovert, since introverts tend to master the art of listening. But it's a balancing act. If you are too introverted, sometimes you can be the one who listens without others realizing it. The goal is that people should understand that you are listening, and they should want to listen to you.

Learn from your models

When a conversation really works, it can be magical. You will surely have experienced such meetings. You talked for four hours, but if felt like four minutes. Afterwards you are surprised and happy at the same time! Conversational geniuses are pleasant and successful people. They make interviews fun regardless of whether they are looking for a job or are the people doing the interviewing. People who master the art of conversation are better positioned for success in life. Good conversation is the link that connects us with others. Studies have shown that children of parents who are good at conversation have a higher IQ. In addition, these children found it easier to meet people and make friends.

The British psychologist Professor Nicholas Humphrey has carried out studies that show that good conversationalists also tend to have a well-tuned ability to see the perspectives of others. Talk-show hosts like Larry King, Oprah Winfrey, Michael Parkinson and Ellen DeGeneres master this. They achieve the goal of getting the guest to talk, and to want to talk.

In all rhetorical situations it is good to study models (*copia*). It is not a question of copying somebody's jargon, but of studying it and then making it your own. If a person who you view as a desirable role model uses humour as a means, you shouldn't copy the jokes, but decide to make use of humour as a tool. So, let us study the conversation models in your everyday life. Think of somebody at your workplace or a friend whom you and many others like to talk to. What is it that makes it such fun to converse with that person?

By studying others, and especially those who get others to talk, understand and listen, you will yourself become a better conversationalist. Learn from them. There are several common denominators among good conversationalists. Let's have a closer look at them.

Open and closed questions

For a successful conversation, the goal is to get the other person to want to talk. Discreetly find out what he or she is interested in. Follow up with questions. If you find common denominators, deepen the conversation around those. Questions – not just idle talk – will spark a conversation. But there are different types of questions. Not all questions are good. Some have the opposite effect – subjects that are far too personal, or that make the other individual feel uncomfortable, for example. So be sure not to ask uncomfortable follow-up questions, forcing the other person to say, "I don't want to talk about that." If the question is uncomfortable, you will see how the person puts a hand up towards their throat. The questions also are of importance for the length of the conversation. There is a difference between open and closed questions. Closed questions lead to short conversations. A typical such question is, 'Do you like Italy?'

The likely answer will be 'Yes' or 'No'. So it is important not to stop there but to go on and follow it with an open question. 'What is it that you like about Italy?' Open questions require an explanation and automatically get the person to talk more.

If the person nevertheless doesn't start talking, you have at least got some important information – the person doesn't want to talk to you. It takes two to tango. But with open questions the likelihood increases that you will have a more lively conversation. To show that you haven't been offended, you can end by saying, "Have a nice evening", "I hope the coffee tastes good, see you around!", or something similar that suits the situation. If you yourself want to indicate that your don't want to talk, then 'Yes' and 'No' answers are simple markers, regardless of whether you're being asked open or closed questions.

How you get the listener to feel that you understand

In the previous chapter, I briefly mentioned rapport. It can be as simple as me looking sad when you tell me something unpleasant with an unhappy look on your face. By doing that, I establish the feeling in you that I understand. The absolute opposite of this is to smile during a sad story – anti-rapport. Then the direct consequence is that you don't think I understand you. To find yourself in anti-rapport, or to have a lack of flow in the conversation, often happens without you being aware of it. And of course the other person will lose confidence. It can be when you move closer despite the fact that the other person has taken a step back, or when your eyes wander. It is difficult to pull off a good meeting with such people; they often suffer from a social handicap. But it is possible to learn how to bridge the gap.

Mirror the other person's body language as well as you can. Examine it discreetly and reflect it back to them. If the listener leans backwards, you do the same, but rather discreetly. If the listener looks worried, you do the same even if you don't know why. But it is even better if you ask, "Are you worried?" with the same expression that the listener has. Then you will be regarded as extremely sensitive. Small tricks can have great effects.

I achieved rapport with a rather manipulative woman I worked with a long time ago. She used dramatic language, which was hard to mirror. And she was regarded as incredibly charming and irresistible by her colleagues. She fired off dazzling white smiles and complements right and left, with a dynamic body language. There was just one catch – the complements were connected to tasks. A common domination technique is called the compliment method. It's always difficult to say thank you for these types of compliments because you've been steered into carrying out a task that the compliment terrorist wrapped it in. One day, this woman was rushing around in the corridors. She seemed stressed and complained about her situation. (Refer to the martyr method I describe in the chapter on how to say awkward things in a nice way). She approached my office and I felt well prepared for her compliment method, this time armoured with a 'thank you' and a mirroring. She swept into my office with a swing of her hips, fired off her smile and gave me that look, the look that made you feel so special, the chosen one. At that moment I was alone in the office and she had no one else to target. I fired a smile back at her, leaned forward and made it look as if I was bursting with expectation.

"Elaiiiine, you who are so charming, sociable and amusing, can you be in charge of the staff meeting this afternoon?" she said, extending an open palm towards me as if she was offering me something really exclusive. I held my hand, palm up, the same way. I was going to give her something just as 'exclusive' back. She looked at my hand, not quite sure what to expect. "How nice that you think I'm charming, sociable and amusing," I said with a smile. "I haven't got time! But thanks!"

My colleague quickly raised her hand to a wave and looked even happier. "Okaaay," she said and neatly swung out of the office. I remained sitting there on my chair, amazed. Could it really be so simple to achieve rapport? Had she really understood? I heard her heels clatter in satisfaction down the corridor, but they slowed when the penny dropped. Then I heard her heels start to come back. I straightened my back and smiled. The next second, she poked her head into my office. She looked rather surprised.

"You said no, didn't you?"

"Exactly," I said, and smiled. She smiled somewhat uncertainly and said okay. I had achieved rapport and taken over the role as compliment dominator at the same time. A dangerous balancing act, that. But the point is that by mirroring body language you can plant a feeling in the listener that you understand and have absorbed what they are saying.

To achieve rapport, you can also read the atmosphere and adapt to it. Is it going to be a jokey sort of meeting, relaxed, or a focused, strictly professional one? Get a feel for the atmosphere and the jargon, and follow it. Look at all the listeners and analyse their mood. Follow with the flow. Meet them where they are and then take them to your destination if you want, and when you want. This is very important to think about when you are mingling. Don't just tramp into a circle of people, but rather glide in smoothly by following their conversation and mood. When people are mingling, it is of course important that you also open up for the person who wants to join in. The atmosphere is not always what one could hope for, and then it can be necessary to steer it in a different direction. But always start by trying to establish rapport.

I once held a rhetoric course for a department where all the employees had found out – the previous day – they were going to lose their jobs. When I entered the room, 40 rather down-hearted gentlemen sat there. One gave me a brave attempt at a smile when I stepped in. And I felt how he tried to apologise for the sad mood. A smile from my side had not fitted in here – that was my destination later – but first I needed to meet my listeners. I didn't take on the role of course leader straight away; rather I was simply Elaine who had just heard the bad news.

"I heard about the news you received yesterday," I began, and some of them looked up (because I was meeting them in their situation). "I want to say how sorry I am."

That sufficed. That I took a little step towards them led to them take several steps towards me. They left their situation and stepped into the world of rhetoric for the simple reason that I had stepped into their world first. It needn't be harder than that. By doing this, you will find it easier to create goodwill in your listener.

Nicholos Boothman recommends three stages of engaging with others: 1) be clear as to which relationship you want to have with the listener 2) evaluate what sort of relationship you get 3) change your manner until you get the relationship you want to have.

Conversation starters
'Do you come here often?'
'So, what do you otherwise do?'
'Where are you from?'

There are countless successful – and less successful – ways to start a conversation. I am sure you will have heard a lot of them. Trying to find a common denominator is always a safe bet. But if you want the person to feel comfortable, you should find a subject that brings a sparkle to her eyes and makes her talk. And if you want the listener to give you information, there are some good tricks you might try. One is that you decide the direction of the conversation by giving information you yourself want, in your own presentation of yourself. Say that you are at a party, and you see a person you want to have contact with. And you also want to know what his relationship is to the hostess:

"Hi, I'm Sandra. I'm an old school mate of Wendy's."

"Mickey. Wendy and I work together."

All you need do is introduce yourself and say what your relationship to the hostess is, and the other person will do the same. The person will follow your introduction pattern for the simple reason that you started – and then it is you who sets the rules. Without thinking, we follow social patterns in introduction situations. And the first person who introduces himself sets the norm for others who follow. If, for example, a work team is attending training and the first person says, "Hi, my name in Anders, I'm an engineer at and I have four children," the next person will say the same: "Hi, Mickey is my name, I work on the assembly line and don't have any children."

I take part in many training courses every year and this is a pattern I see again and again. If one person delivers a long monologue, then the others do too. Sometimes I have experimented a little to see if the others follow the pattern even if it is a little bizarre: "Hi, I am Elaine, I am a rhetorician, 29 years old, but mentally I am more like 43 years old." That introduction was not just a conversation starter, but also an icebreaker that aroused quite a lot of laughter and curiosity as to what the others would say. When they follow your example, the conversation is up and going. And all you need to do is follow up with open questions. 'What do you work with?', 'How long have you done that?', 'What did you want to be from the start?' Try to start with something that gets the other person to talk. But avoid the old clichés: 'Do you come here often?' or 'Where are you from?' They can make people think you are boring and have nothing interesting to say.

Dare to deepen the conversation

It is a question of balancing the conversation, and not ending up in vapid talk about the weather, nor revealing everything. It might just happen that you meet your soul mate and feel that you can expose your entire life. But that is rare. Let's stick to the middle of the conversation scale. Test by saying something that arouses the listener's attention and curiosity. For example, 'Shall we skip the small talk and simply expose our prejudices? You can start. How do you think I voted in the last election?' Make sure you say this in a light tone so you don't frighten the listener off.

To get to know a person, it can be a good idea to talk about things that reveal values. To do that, you can describe hypothetical scenarios. To create a more comfortable mood you can choose a simple one. 'If you could be a celebrity for one day, who would you choose?' These can sound like banal conversation starters, but they can lead to quite a lot of interesting discussions. That is why the subject of philosophy remained of interest for more than 2,000 years – there is always something to discuss, and you can't arrive at an absolute truth. But you can find out what the other person thinks. And above all, the conversation flows.

Take a stand

There are those who strive for maximum harmony and never take a stand for or against anything in front of others. They are often green people. But sometimes discussions arise where people want to hear your viewpoint and the motivation behind it. To answer, 'I don't know' or 'I don't dare answer' is regarded as meaningless, boring and – above all – stingy, since you don't want to contribute with your thoughts the same way others contribute. A conversation is a lot of give and take, so don't forget to give.

Looking at everybody

If you are in a bigger setting, look at everybody. Otherwise you run the risk of being regarded as unsympathetic. When I wrote the book *Domination Technique,* I received emails from many managers who described how tiresome it was to be with employees who only looked at them, never at one another.

"They were the people I trusted the least," a participant told me in at an *Inspiring Leadership* course I hold every year. "That is arse kissing. And it reveals a person who doesn't understand that teamwork doesn't only depend on the team captain but also on all the members of the team. Those who create alliances with each other are also typical people who work against you instead of with you." So forget that bit about checking the key person. *Everybody* is your key person.

Listening

> *"I remind myself every morning: Nothing I say this day will teach me anything. So, if I'm going to learn, I must do it by listening."* – Larry King

The key is to be interested for real. To listen. The American TV presenter Larry King often manages to talk somebody down, but also to get them to talk. He summarises the key to his success in the above quote. The words he uses to have a good conversation are the same words that his interviewee uses.

Listening is a key to the art of conversation. That is where the monologue monsters fail. Many people think that such monsters have an easy time taking what they want, and are thus social geniuses. But, if you can't balance talking with listening, there will be no dialogue. If you yourself are a monologue monster, it might be because you repeat too much of what is said to you. You draw parallels to your own life and the people you know. Avoid that. Resist the temptation to drag the other person into your domains. Stay in the world that the person who is talking wants to share. Try to understand it. Ask resulting questions. And to listen optimally you should try to visualize what the other person says. That will make it harder for you to float away in your own thoughts, as well as making what you hear more real. If there is something you don't understand, say so and ask the person to explain. That is simply proof that you are paying attention and want to understand. You will still have the chance to have your say (as long as you are not sitting next to a monologue monster), and then hopefully you will be asked resulting questions.

Picking up the details

I got to learn a thing or two from Norway's most sought-after doctor, Jörgen Skavlan (elder brother of Fredrik Skavlan of the TV talk show). We had an interesting conversation about the importance of conversation technique as part of a professional role. Jörgen was named as the most popular doctor in Norway in 2008. How did he become that? Earlier in the decade Norway introduced a model in primary health care that allowed patients to choose their doctor. And Jörgen is the doctor that most Norwegians have as their first choice. What is the secret? Jörgen himself says that it is conversation technique – the art of taking people the right way. I met him at an event in Bodö, northern Norway, where we both lectured.

"A lot of doctors think they work with medicine, but they forget that they are treating individuals," he told me. "The link between us and those individuals is communication. That's why it is strange that the people who want to become doctors are only expected to have very good school grades – it is only in Ireland that administrators who select those who are admitted to medical school check whether the applicants are good people too."

Lotta Gray, who is the author of the blog 'Vimmelmamman' [Bewildered mum] where she writes about her life with cancer, confirms what Jörgen says: "I have had four doctors, but have not bonded with any of them. I attend an appointment and am not allowed to be Lotta, but am forced to be a patient. I would like to meet a doctor who doesn't just see my cancer but also sees me and my life. It can be as simple as asking about my son Lennox."

So what is the secret behind so many people wanting to have Jörgen as their doctor? Sure, he is a good conversationalist and he is without doubt a competent doctor, but what did he actually do that makes the difference? The answer is that he listened and picked up details from the patient's life that he subsequently entered in their medical records. When other doctors saw the notes, they laughed. There were items such as 'yacht', 'old cat' and other things that the patient had mentioned to Jörgen. And that was the key to his good relationship with the patient. He has more than 2,300 patients and there was no way he could keep track of all of them through sheer memory. But before meeting each patient he looked in his notes. Then he started the meeting not by talking about medicine, but about the patient. 'How are you doing with your yacht?' The fact that Jörgen knew about the patient's leisure activities and life created goodwill and confidence.

So, to be able to continue to have successful conversations with the same person, connect them with a detail and start the next conversation with that. You will make an impression. You will show that the last time you didn't just make idle chat but really took in what that person said. To take in a name is impressive, but to take in details is immensely so.

Types of jargon to avoid

The know-it-all tries to appear clever, but is not listened to. There is something repulsive about people who might indeed know better, but who want you to feel much worse than them. They are superior and other people have to pay for it. They tend to start by using your given name and stretching it: 'Elaineeee, you see it's like this…' If you have been irritated by somebody who's used your given name it is probably a perfectly justifiable feeling. Politicians can look really haughty on TV when they say, 'But, Fredrik Reinfeldt…' even though it is a vicious debate. When an adult says your given name to correct you, it arouses irritation. After all, you are no longer five years old. What happens is that the goodwill instantly disappears. You stop listening. Your inner voice has woken up and says unpleasant things about the know-it-all. The feelings that have been aroused will of course depend on the context. Sometimes it can be affectionate. But in connection with criticism, or correction, it is not a hit.

Sometimes the person who is going to correct you will start with a 'but'. They'll lean their head to one side and put their hand *considerately* on your shoulder. 'But Elaine…' The know-it-alls also explain things that are obvious, and they make a point of emphasizing them while looking intently at you to make sure you're really following. But what they are actually doing is making sure that you feel really stupid.

Know-it-alls only manage to express their message, but never to get it to sink in, since their personality does not arouse goodwill. If the listener does not like you, he or she will rarely hear what you have to say. Anyway, the likelihood is that you are going to say something that the other person doesn't like.

Using sarcasm is also risky, especially if people don't know you. Sarcasm is when words and tone don't harmonize. If your words don't match your body language, or tone, then the listener might respond based on your body language and tone. The problem is you can never be completely certain.

So avoid these types of jargon. Strive instead to get a black belt in conversation technique. If a conversation went really badly, don't settle for that. Don't think, 'This person didn't understand anything at all.' That won't make it better. Memorize what you said and create a better version of the conversation, mentally. Try to improve on that the next time you talk with the same person, and carry the following list in your head.

Check list for black belt in conversation technique:

- Use open questions
- Find smart conversation starters and take the lead – 'Hi, I'm Sandra, I'm an old school friend of Wendy's
- Deepen the conversation – talking about the weather isn't interesting for very long
- Find common denominators
- Find the subject that sparks off your listener and makes them want to go on talking about it
- Look at everybody in the conversation group
- Listen
- Pick up on details
- Avoid sarcasm, irony and looking at your watch or smartphone

Chapter

The art of
persuasion -
argumentation
techniques

A married couple went on holiday. In the afternoon, the husband wanted to have a nap. His wife decided to go on a little trip with the boat. She piloted the boat out into the bay, dropped anchor and pulled out a book. When she was deeply absorbed in the book, a security guard appeared in his boat. He stopped next to the woman and said:

"Good morning, madam! What are you doing?"

"I'm reading a book," she answered, while she thought that he ought to be able to see that.

"There are fishing restrictions here," he informed her.

"Yes, that's possible... but I'm not fishing, I'm reading."

"But you have fishing equipment in the boat. As far as I know, you could start any minute. I must take you back to the station and write a report."

"For reading?" the woman asked, perplexed.

"Yes, there are fishing restrictions here."

"But I'm not fishing, I'm reading."

"Indeed, but you have the equipment for it, so you could start any minute," the guard repeated, and waved the woman towards him.

"If you do that," she said, "I will be forced to report you for sexual harassment."

"But I haven't touched you," said the guard, who now had a worried look on his face.

"That's true, but you have the equipment for it. As far as I know, you can start any minute."

"Have a nice day, madam!" said the guard, as he quickly moved away.

A lot of people misunderstand argumentation techniques. They think that you should win the argument. That is correct, but you want to win the person over to your side. People who master argumentation technique leave their opponent speechless, with an open mouth and a feeling that their antagonist was right. This applies to negotiation technique as well. You shouldn't just steam-roll somebody. You should win the other person over to your side. The woman in the boat wanted the guard to just get the hell out of there and leave her to read in peace. She could have said, 'Leave me alone!' or 'You're a ridiculous pedant who can't think for yourself.' Instead, she made a quick recipient adaptation and applied the same principle to the guard that he had applied to her. If she had started verbally assaulting him, or tried to convince him she was right, she would not have achieved the same result that she did with argumentation technique, which is getting people to do and think what you want them to.

To put it bluntly, a person who uses argumentation techniques can tell somebody to go to hell and at the same time get them to look forward to the journey. To win supporters, you shouldn't fawn on those who already think the same as you. You *can* do that to keep them on your side, but you should concentrate your effort on those who don't share your views. This chapter teaches you how to persuade and to get others to think like you.

Bear in mind the following when you start to persuade people in your everyday life:

He who doesn't think like you is not necessarily your enemy, he just needs different arguments to be persuaded.

What those arguments are, we shall very soon go into, but first a few things should be made clear. Argumentation techniques are not just for politicians. They are relevant for you in your work life and in private. They are negotiation and selling techniques, and that is what we do every day when we try to get people to think like us and have the same views as us. You can study politicians if you like, but they will not make you a better negotiator. Politicians tend to call each other by their given names and surnames. They shake their heads when the other person is talking and say, "You haven't understood anything!" Imagine if you did that with your boss when trying to negotiate your salary – making a face, shaking your head, and saying, "But, you haven't understood a thing!" That won't be a successful negotiation.

Politicians ought to try and negotiate their way to more voters by offering better proposals for their country instead of scorning their opponents. More about that later. This leads me to an important point, and an attitude that you should assume in your argumentation techniques.

The listener is not your enemy

People with views that are opposed to yours just need to change their perspective. And you are the guide to lead the way for them. So do it nicely! No screwed-up eyes, no ignoring of questions, no scornful comments – just nice guidance. Nobody is going to follow a guide who gives them the finger. Others have neither seen nor heard what you have seen and heard. So it isn't so strange that they don't think the same as you. And vice versa. The most important ingredient in trying to convince others is the ability to change perspective. Few people dare do this, for fear of themselves changing opinion.

There are historical and more topical examples that show how badly it works if you regard people with opposite views as enemies. Malcolm X and Martin Luther King both struggled for the rights of black people, but Malcolm X also waved his finger at the enemy, whom he called 'the white man'. Martin Luther King instead pointed his index finger towards the future and said, "I have a dream." In 2010, we saw how the media ran campaigns against Swedish Democrats [the extreme, right-wing populist party], something that probably also gained them sympathy votes. You don't achieve your purpose by, for example, ranting on about how you hate the Swedish Democrats, or any other party. You achieve it by listening to them. Study their arguments and then put forward better arguments. Prime Minister Fredrik Reinfeldt expressed this skilfully when he said, "I don't want to spend time on the Swedish Democrats, but I do want to listen to their voters."

Goodwill means that people who have not yet seen the light will more easily move over to your side. If they don't like you, then it doesn't matter how good an argument you have. Adopt that attitude from the very beginning: people who aren't on your side have just gone slightly astray.

For (pro), or against (contra)?

To start with, you need to think about whether you are *for* something (pro) or *against* it (contra). The most successful persuaders don't talk about what they are against. Instead, they always have a proposal with nuances that attract the listener. But there are examples of the opposite. The Swedish Democrats are against mass immigration and they are against what they call 'Islami-sation' in Sweden. If we return to Malcolm X, the greater part of his argumentation was also based on contra-argumentation. He not only struggled for the rights of black people, he was actively against 'the white man'. A lot of his rhetoric built upon the anger he felt against those who oppressed blacks.

"Usually when people are sad, they don't do anything," he said in 1965. "They just cry over their condition. But when they get angry, they bring about a change."

A contra-argumentation often requires a polemic – two different sides to choose from. It is OK to have the good and the bad. For the Sweden Democrats, pensioners were the good ones, and immigrants the bad ones. For Malcolm X, black people were the good ones, and the whites bad. It wasn't difficult to be a Malcolm X supporter in those days – black people were burnt alive on crosses, beaten up by the police, forced to sit at the back of the bus just because they had the wrong skin colour. It was easy to point at the problem, as it was so obvious. The problem was racism and the racists were the whites. But the trap with that argumentation was that it created a polemic between whites and blacks, which led to many blacks themselves becoming racists. We saw the same phenomenon in Sweden in 2010. The Sweden Democrats were named and shamed. Many peopled froze them out and there were mass demonstrations. People broke with those they personally knew and were close to, who happened to be supporters of the party. The same segregation and discrimination that the Swedish Democrats were criticised for was applied to them.

Hatred always benefits the opposite party because they can make use of martyrdom. Examples of contra-argumentation's starting point:

'I am against…'
'We shall not…'
'Beware of…'

If you want to use rhetoric to get a group to support you, you should use pro-argumentation. This leaves a good feeling with the listeners since you have a proposal that benefits them. Just like the message should be made attractive for the listener, even the opinion you want to persuade them about should be made attractive. Pro-argumentation proposes a goal you want to reach. So your first question before you start building up your argument should always be, 'What is my proposal?' The proposal is the thesis. That is, the statement upon which you build up your entire argumentation. You need to be crystal clear for your own sake, then you won't risk seeming vague. Now think about what your proposal is. It doesn't need to be a political position; it can be something that palpably affects your everyday life. Perhaps you are going to go on a trip with your partner, or ask your boss to raise your salary. Whatever it is, the first step is to formulate it positively:

'I would like…'
'My proposal is…'
'What is going to make a real, positive difference is…'
'My goal is…'

Now, when you have the proposal clear in your mind, you can't make the mistake of leading 'the people who have gone astray' down the wrong path. You are certain about the destination. And that means it will feel safe for them to follow along with you.

Now it is time to list the arguments, and to move on towards your goal. But, first, an argument technique you should avoid is starting out with, 'I think…' Nobody, not a single person, is interested in what you think… unless you yourself are the goal. The recipient will always wonder how he will benefit by following you, as with the earlier phone salesman example. The focus should not be on your views. That will just make the listener sceptical. A skilful telephone salesperson rarely says that they think a particular model is fantastic. He puts forward arguments that make you come to that conclusion. The same happens in a clothes shop. They say, "That looks really nice on you," but only when they notice that you really like it yourself, just to give us that little extra push. The point, and the hidden proposal, is, 'Do your shopping here!' It also means that we leave the shop with somewhat lighter steps, and not just because we have emptied our wallet. And, we will be happy to go back there again, since it felt so easy to shop there. Formulate your arguments so that they encourage the listener to spontaneously adopt your values and goals.

Three arguments suffice. If you have more, the listener will think you are desperate. If you have less, he or she will wonder if that was all you had to say.

A classic disposition in the art of argumentation is to think 'two, one, three' or 'medium-strength, weak, strong'. The first argument you have should be the middle-strength one of the three. The second should be the weakest. Then the listener will begin to think critically and think that this wasn't such a big deal. But then you come back with your strongest argument. That is the final thrust and the one that the listener will take with them.

When it comes to the content of the argument, it is important that you have a balance between ethos, logos and pathos arguments. Some people think that it is enough to list a whole lot of figures and statistics to convince a listener. Logos-arguments are indeed extremely important. But they should be a part of the three arguments. Bring forth your own experiences to strengthen the listener's conviction.

Ethos arguments are important because we want to see the proposal in context, and it is always more convincing if you've been there, seen and experienced the consequences of what you are arguing for. Then the listener will want to know what he gains from thinking the same as you, and that is where the pathos argument comes in. Draw up an argument that affects the feelings of those who are listening.

In what order should these arguments come? That depends. If you have an audience that loves figures, then of course you should end with a logos argument. If you have more of a feeling audience, end with the pathos argument. Vary this, depending on who you want to convince. There are many different groups, so the order will never be self-evident, but the important thing is to end forcefully and strongly. The after-taste when the other person has heard your argumentation ought to be a heavy one. But, so that he won't become suspicious, you must show him that you have been on the 'other side' and weighed and pondered the arguments *against* your position – and despite that you've managed to hold on to your conviction.

The argument from hell (refutatio)

If you are to appear objective without intentions, you ought to show your listener that you have perspective. Before you bring out the strongest argument you should take up the counter argument from hell, *refutatio* as the Greeks called it. That is the strongest argument against your proposal. "But that sounds utterly crazy, you can't take that up," say many clients when I coach them in rhetoric prior to their giving a presentation to a critical audience. But that is precisely what you should do! Then the listener gets the impression that you are with them, and that you see the pitfalls they see. When they have grasped that, they will be willing to buy your last strong argument that the proposal rests upon. We like those who see things the way we do. Let me give you examples of people who dealt with the question from hell.

Barack Obama won the Nobel Peace Prize in 2009. At the time, as the President of the United States, he had responsibility for three wars. The world turned up its nose and from East to West expressed dissatisfaction. Others laughed and began to think that the Nobel committee was a joke. Obama travelled to Norway to receive his prize. The argument from hell had been, "Obama does not deserve the prize because he is responsible for three ongoing wars." Obama began his speech by saying that he didn't deserve the prize. Because he was sufficiently open in acknowledging what everyone saw, it became reasonable to think that he did deserve a prize. (Perhaps not the Nobel Peace Prize, but even so…) He re-defined the prize as an encouragement to continue to work for peace. By doing so he saved not only his face, but also that of the Nobel committee.

Estate agents should also need to use *refutatio*. They have a lot of arguments for why you should buy the property they are selling, and as a sort of occupational hazard they use far too many superlatives. But they forget the catch. They should proactively mention the downsides and disadvantages that people can see and turn them into something positive. 'The kitchen is rather small, but the wall is not structural so it can be pulled down to create a much larger kitchen that extends into the living room,' for instance. Those who don't mention the catch leave people wondering what it is. You don't want that to happen.

Refutatio is necessary. The person who gives a picture of themselves as being without fault is not credible. If you don't tell the truth yourself, somebody else will, and it will take on greater proportions. The TV host David Letterman understood this in October 2009. When his reputation couldn't be argued against, he publicly apologised. He told his viewers the truth about his mistresses, apologised and was forgiven. Those who admit the truth too late have a worse time (Tiger Woods and Bill Clinton). So, if you have done something stupid that could be revealed, be the one to tell people first, so that nobody else can. More about this in the chapter on saying troublesome things nicely.

It is important to study the enemy, by which I mean those whose views are the complete opposite of yours. That is how you win them over to your side. Nelson Mandela studied his enemies over the course of 27 years in prison. He learned what they were passionate about. What they read and how they thought. That was a powerful weapon to disarm them when he stepped out into freedom. "If you want to make peace with your enemy, you have to work with your enemy," he said. "Then he will become your partner."

In argumentation technique it is important to study the counter-argument just as carefully as your own. If someone is your enemy, you shouldn't point your finger at them. You should study them or talk with them. Find out what they think and try to find out the most compelling argument they have against you. Then you have found *refutatio*, which you subsequently raise in your argumentation to win over their supporters to your side. After that, you nail it with your third argument. So the disposition of the arguments should be: medium-strong argument, weak argument, counter argument/*refutatio* and strong argument.

Not everyone dares to converse with the enemy. There are, after all, ample risks. You stand there, either armed with too much ammunition, or you become less aggressive because you are starting to understand them. Few people risk the latter. But to critically examine the enemy's arguments can sometimes be an examination of your own (something that people with crazy views would benefit by doing).

Try it yourself!

Is there something you really would like to convince somebody about? Perhaps you want to persuade your partner to make dinner. Or a lazy colleague to do their job. Try to present cooking dinner as a 'possibility'. I realise that I am stepping into a minefield here for the opponents of domination techniques. But sometimes the difference between argumentation techniques and manipulation can be very subtle. The idea is not that you should deviously manipulate somebody – you should persuade them. With rhetoric as a means, you should always be as truthful as possible, even though it is hard to convey the truth since it is relative. You can only give your truth. But you should always aspire to the truth. The Roman orator Quintilianus talked about how one should be a good man, in the context that led to one becoming a perfect orator (*vir bonus*). He emphasized that it was a lofty ideal that couldn't be reached, but which one should always aspire to. It is the same with argumentation techniques, and thus with rhetoric.

I am lazy and I love sweets. I think I have achieved something if I briefly grace the gym with my presence. I don't even have to lift any weights, or touch a treadmill – I have 'been to the gym'. That is why I now have a personal trainer (David Englund) who I am, thank God, unable to talk down. He has a black belt in argumentation techniques and always manages to transform difficult things into a 'possibility'. And that is necessary – not least for rhetoricians. I could perhaps get a trainer to give me less work by playing the martyrdom card. But David turns a blind eye to that. He listens to my body and sees how much it can manage. It can sound something like this when I have a 40-kilo bar on my neck and am going to do a squat: "Elaine, now you shall do ten squats in a row with perfect depth and the right technique. If you don't do them perfectly, you have the *possibility* to do them again."

We both know that is a nice way of saying: "Elaine, now you *must* do ten perfect squats in a row and if you don't do them properly, then you *must* do them again." But that version would be intimidation rhetoric, which I will deal with later in this book.

I promised earlier that I would describe how I persuaded my husband that we should travel to Brazil for the fifth year in a row. Now that we have children it is slightly more difficult, but it's still feasible.

Proposal: Our winter journey will be to Brazil.

Medium-strength argument: Ethos, which suits Gustav: We've been there before, after all, and every time you have been so happy that we decided to travel there again and again.

Weak argument: Logos, since it is hard to find statistics that say that travellers are satisfied with Brazil: Four out of four times, we have been satisfied with the journey.

Refutatio: Perhaps you think we should go somewhere else since we have been to Brazil four times.

Strong argument: Pathos: Our son is 25% Brazilian, so it is important that he doesn't miss that culture in his life.

Is the strong argument a cheap trick? Could be, but it works!

What do you want to convince your listeners about? Write down your proposal. Then list the arguments, name the counter-arguments and end with the strongest argument. Make sure that they are ethos, pathos and logos arguments. See what happens:

Proposal:
Argument 2:
Argument 1:
Refutatio:
Argument 3:

Win new supporters!

To get as many people as possible to think like you, it is important not to concentrate solely on those who agree with you. Of course it is much nicer to say what you think to those who are on the same wavelength. But they are already believers. The question is: How are you going to win over the others, the non-believers, and still retain your old supporters? As I wrote earlier, the Swedish Moderate Party tried to win Social Democrats over to their side. They used the word 'new' and linked that with the moderate party. Then they made their logo light blue, not red, nor the former party blue, but quite simply light blue. A smart move. If they had gone too far, they would have lost supporters. There was a lot of strategy from the [non-socialist] Alliance side. And the Social Democrats countered with arguments like: 'The problem is not that you call yourself old or new conservatives, the problem is that you *are* conservatives.' Ultimately, the Social Democrats suffered the worst election results in their history.

When we rhetoric consultants analyse politicians, we are often obliged to take up the subtle and obvious insults that most of them fling at their their opponents. They try to sink them verbally, often with mudslinging rhetoric. The problem is that this is entirely the wrong way to win votes and supporters. There is nothing new about the fact that politicians represent different sections of the population in the town, region or country they represent. If, say, the politician Mona Sahlin shakes her head when she looks at her rival Reinfeldt, ignores his questions and heaps scorn on his proposals, then she ignores and heaps scorn on the people he represents as well. That is why as a politician (or a businessman, or whatever you are) you should never sink those who don't share your views – you should sink their argument.

When you think in terms of argumentation techniques, think of politicians in a debate and do the exact opposite. Don't sink your opponent. Sink your opponent's arguments, and you will win their supporters over to your side. Study positive examples too. Dare to go outside the political sphere. Rhetoric stretches far beyond just politics. Take, for example, a really good pop song – a tune that makes you think and reflect. We will find argumentation techniques in that.

I often mention Michael Jackson's *Man in the Mirror* as an example of brilliant argumentation techniques. He starts the song by clearly explaining his thesis, which is positively formulated. You will benefit from doing as Jackson suggests in *Man in the Mirror*, because it will feel good and right for you.

> *I'm gonna make a change*
> *For once in my life*
> *It's gonna feel real good*
> *Gonna make a difference*
> *Gonna make it right...*

He doesn't point at anybody else. He points at himself. He wants everyone to make a difference, and starts with himself in the first words he utters. Michael tells us how it is going to feel good and says it's going to be right; the very thesis is formulated so that you will find it attractive. But the thesis must stand on arguments. Why should he make a difference? He starts with an ethos argument, things he has seen and experienced himself that strengthen his thesis.

I see the kids in the streets with not enough to eat
Who am I to be blind pretending not to see their needs

He is going to make a difference because children are starving. And if you don't see that, you are blind. So he creates a subtle polemic: either you see the reality, or you are blind to it. He even combines the other argument with *refutatio*. Michael lived a life of luxury, which was the counter-argument to why he should care. And he answers that contradiction like this:

I've been a victim of a selfish kind of love
It's time that I realize
There are some with no home
Not a nickel to loan

And finally he comes to the third argument, which is a combination of pathos and logos arguments – the fact that there are homeless people. He tells of the reality of children's lives to motivate us to do what he proposes in the refrain.

They follow the pattern of the wind yasee
Cause they got no place to be
That's why I'm starting with me!

The rhetoric of music is effective. You can get people to 'sing your message' if you give them a catchy melody (I shall go into this later). And with argumentation that is as clear as a bell you can get them not only to say what you want, but also to think it. With his hit *Man in the Mirror*, Michael Jackson got a whole world to sing what he wanted them to do – see themselves in the mirror and go out and make a difference. The refrain was the thesis for his argumentation. And he got a whole world to sing his thesis.

I'm starting with the man in the mirror
I'm asking him to change his ways
And no message could have been any clearer
If you wanna make the world a better place
Take a look at yourself and then make a change

So genuine argumentation technique is not just listing your arguments. It is also about getting others in their turn to want to list them. There is a difference between persuading and convincing. If you persuade somebody, the listener does what you want unwillingly. If you convince them, you have achieved the goal of your argumentation: to arouse interest, create understanding, win approval and elicit a reaction.

Intimidation rhetoric (argumentum ad baculum)

How do you, as a leader, get a member of your staff to move towards 'the light' when everything looks so dark? During an economic crisis, the boss can either motivate by pointing his finger at the goal, or he can threaten with the edge of a cliff. Some use intimidation rhetoric. They subtly threaten their staff with consequences if, for example, they run over their budget. That creates a climate where nobody wants to shoulder responsibility since the leader has clearly articulated what the consequences will be. Who wants to work there?

I worked at just such a place. I thought of the company's two dynamic leaders as 'compliment Hitlers'. They dished out compliments right and left – and that might sound nice – but there was a catch. Every compliment came hand-in-hand with a task. The employees were manipulated into doing what the bosses wanted. The result was a subtle whip that led to people putting in overtime and ending up on sick leave long after the company went bankrupt.

The world's leading motivation researcher, Professor Edward Deci, has consistently demonstrated how compliments and praise, when they are used as tools for controlling, have the completely opposite effect on people's will and commitment than what was intended. Praise and encouragement should, according to Deci, only be used for the purpose of confirming and reinforcing… not to convey demands, wishes and expectations.

To whip your staff into success is like whipping your company to ruin. And wrapping the whip in diplomatic euphemisms doesn't make any difference – it is still intimidation rhetoric. Politicians make exactly the same mistake when they point at their opponents instead of winning over their opponents' supporters with the help of pro-argumentation, which helps spotlight their goals.

So, those who use intimidation rhetoric say, "It is best that you train hard so you won't be fat next summer." Others motivate and encourage you to train: "You're going to be in really great shape next summer." It is not unusual for intimidation rhetoric to be used without thinking in a child's upbringing: "Be careful so you don't drop the glass." That can create an image for the child that actually results in them dropping the glass. Instead, you should plants positive images. "How clever you are at holding the glass!" Then it is a hidden exhortation, without intimidation. Intimidation rhetoric differs from positive theses. A positively formulated proposal is, for example: "Rhetoric is the path to success." The equivalent, which I call intimidation rhetoric, is: "Lack of rhetoric is the path to ruin." With the latter, only negative follow-up questions are formed, and these intimidate supporters. Intimidation rhetoric can work when it comes, for example, to the importance of using seat belts in your car. Then it is a negation exhortation: "Don't forget to fasten your seat belt." And the argument for why you should do so is:

1. You can end up with a crushed skull
2. You can seriously injure your passengers
3. You can die

That works with safety belts, but the argument points to potential negative results. Intimidation rhetoric leads to one of the following three responses: the recipient flees, the recipient attacks, or the recipient feels paralyzed. Hitler, unfortunately, used successful intimidation rhetoric to make the German people feel paralyzed which gave him the authority to act himself. But the population acted nevertheless, in the way he wanted – against the Jewish people. The population became afraid of those the intimidator had portrayed as the enemy.

The dilemma that gets others to act

If you want people to act, you can serve them a dilemma: a problem or a situation where a choice has to be made. By that I mean that you should not fool people into thinking that there are two alternatives if in fact there are five. If you do that, you are serving a false dilemma. To avoid that, you should be honest and say that you shall talk about two of the five alternatives. But if there is a distinct general dilemma, such as 'Mac or PC' then there are reasons to talk about the *competing alternative*. In your everyday life you can show that there are choices between a worse and a better. 'Choose the better alternative!' If there is a competitive alternative to your proposal then you can include it in your argumentation – like a lower, or higher, salary. On that point, your employer no doubt thinks that you deserve a low salary because 'there are a lot of costs now'. But you can talk about giving you a raise in terms of an investment in the company's future. If there is a competitive alternative, then you ought to mention it. Apple did that quite successfully in a 2002 campaign that would literally transform the world's vocabulary.

There's the PC, and a slow, overweight man can be seen. Everything in his world seemed to be complicated and difficult. And then there's the Mac, and a lively, handsome nerd in his twenties. He smiles at PC and wonders if they should try and come up with something together.

"I can't," says an obviously tired PC. "I'd have to download this and that, and it would take ages because I'm already completely full!"

"But can't you simply do this?" asks Mac, again smiling at PC, who looks sad because this complicated stuff all sounds so simple for Mac.

"No, then I must do these ten other things first."

Mac shakes his head and leaves. Curtain.

The company succeeded in illustrating Mac and PC users in a humorous manner that many people could recognise. The campaign had such an impact that people started calling themselves a Mac-person or a PC-person. There was a subtle negation thesis, 'Don't buy a PC'. But it was balanced against a proposal: 'Buy a Mac'. It was done with a lot of humour and with a glint in the eye. And it worked!

Take a stand

If you are liked by everybody, the risk is great that you will not be seen by anybody. In argumentation technique it is important to take a clear and decisive stand for something. There is a risk that people won't like what you say, but at least you are taking a stand. If you want to minimise the risk of becoming unpopular, you should avoid negation theses. It isn't hard to work out why they don't work. You don't see IKEA ads that say, 'Don't shop at Habitat' or H&M ads that say, 'Don't shop at Zara, they suck!' You don't see such ads for the simple reason that they don't work. And besides, they risk damaging your brand.

The Swedish Democratic party (SD) are an exception. They chose a negation thesis and that led to success, for the simple reason that the other parties were too busy boasting about Sweden's 'open door' for immigrants but not mentioning the non-existent opportunities for them in the Swedish labour market. SD are against what they call mass immigration and Islamisation.

Negation theses work in the short term, but soon the listener will want you to balance it with a proposal. When I spoke to SD supporters after the election, several said, "I voted for them because I wanted to look after the immigrants we have in Sweden, to help them integrate and get a job. To do that, we can't admit any more of them into the country." That can sound more caring, and to increase their popularity SD could have done as many successful companies have done and used positive theses. 'Burn more calories', 'Let yourself be inspired', 'A delight to drive' instead of negation theses such as 'Stop being fat', 'Stop being uninspired' and 'Avoid crashing your car'. In the book *When you do What I Want* by Henrik Fexeus, he explains that our attitude towards something is governed by how it is described for us. He gives an example with 600 potentially terminally ill people. If they take medicine A, 400 of them will survive, but if they take medicine B, 200 will die. Most people think that medicine A sounds like a better deal, even though both medicines lead to the same result – namely that 400 people live and 200 die. Even the former American First Lady Nancy Reagan managed to get the death penalty to sound like a reasonable alternative with the formulation, 'I believe there would be many people alive today if there were a death penalty!'

So in other words the SD could have said, "We want to take care of our immigrants, integrate them and give them jobs." They might even have won over an immigrant or two by saying, "We're how you get the job you want and the chance to dance with other Swedes around the Midsummer pole." The hidden premise would after all have been, 'Help us to close the door so that more of your mates don't come in'. But, if they had been skilful, they would not have revealed the hidden premise. There are hidden premises everywhere. So the next chapter comes at just the right time.

Chapter

7

Learn to see
through people
and things –
arouse your
inner sceptic

What if everything you have learned up to today was lie? The woman who you fell in love with, the political party you voted for. The party leader you trusted was nothing but a generator of empty phrases. Everything was simply made-up. It's a dreadful thought, isn't it?! Thank God it isn't like that. But you ought to see through the rest. Through the years you have probably already fallen for one thing or another, presumably because you haven't been sufficiently sceptical/curious.

Imagine for a moment that you are going to be subjected to a minimum of 20 lies a day. They could include the next commercial on TV, the next newspaper headline, the clothes shop salesperson, the next conversation with a colleague. Or your partner. We humans are creatures of comfort, so comfortable that it is easier for us to fall for lies than to see through them. Our brain is built upon a system of generalisations. We generalise, as I mentioned earlier, although we are unaware that we're doing so. We would not function without the ability to refine and simplify. So it is sometimes comfortable to accept statements without checking them, but that is dangerous if you just charge ahead.

If, on the other hand, you could learn to see through this and do so without too much effort, wouldn't that be delightful? Yes, I thought you would agree. And that is what this chapter will achieve. It will teach you how to identify the fallacies – the rhetorical pitfalls, the tricks. In my opinion, the art of seeing through other people is one of the most important parts of rhetoric. But it is also important to examine yourself – to see whether your own intentions are evil, whether your argumentation is lacking something. You might even discover that you are wrong. Then a critical attitude can help you to deal with those faults or change your opinion.

There is no absolute truth, just versions of it. Everything is relative. But if the speaker twists things or withholds information, it is important that as many people as possible, preferably everyone, is armed with the ability to think critically. Sceptical, critical thinking should be taught in schools. There's probably a little bit in standard school curricula about a critical attitudes towards sources, but very little. In the book *School for Sceptics* by Andreas Anundi and C J Åkerberg, the sceptic is defined as a person who does not care about prestige. A person who admits they are wrong more often than others. A person without prestige. The sceptic is content with the ability to reconsider their attitude toward this or that, and allow themselves to be wrong sometimes. Do you allow yourself to be wrong? Or have you had the same values over a very long time without reconsidering them? While others stick firmly to their view – regardless of changes in the world around them – the sceptic can see the advantage of discarding old truths.

It can even be dangerous not to question. If you uncritically suck in all information, it becomes more difficult to accept new statements that are contrary to the facts that you have so blindly said yes to. To become a sceptic it is important that: 1) you should not equate personal conviction with facts or truth – a basic sense of relativism is important. 2) you should know that even if something is true *for you*, it can't necessarily be assumed to be a general truth.

You must be sceptical. Not just of yourself but also of others. I am certain you've found yourself stuck in frustrating conversations that are difficult to put your finger on. Like why the telemarketer succeeded in keeping you on the phone a whole minute, even though you wanted to end the call straight away. Or how your boss managed to embellish 'an opportunity', which resulted in your staying on and working late, just because you were given a 'chance'. Wouldn't it be lovely to be able to see through manipulators and charmers? To put your finger on what it is that leads to you finding yourself in their manipulative grip? And so that you will not be regarded as a negative doubter in general, we will make use of a euphemism. Let's sideline the word 'sceptic' and call it 'curious' instead. Being curious has a more positive ring to it (as long as you don't go and poke your nose in too far). Find the balance, but above all find the rhetorical pitfalls.

Start with yourself!

Do you have a view or an opinion that many people are critical of? Write it down. Then it will be easier to see it from a distance. It is important to see your standpoint from a distance to be able to become a full-fledged sceptic. People who connect an opinion to themselves find it harder to change their views, or to be able to critically examine their own values and thoughts. For example, it is harder for somebody who says, "I am a Social Democrat," than for the person who says, "I vote for the Social Democrats." If you want to challenge yourself, choose a standpoint that is connected to you personally. And don't be worried. By critically examining your views, you may end up reinforcing your conviction. If the opposite happens, well that is good too. It is better to change, if what you believed in turned out to be based on weak foundations. Write down your opinion here:

....

....

....

....

....

....

The next step is to see what your opinion is based upon. Ask yourself, 'How do I know about this?' 'How did I find out about it?' 'How do other people know this?' The exact opposite is to say, 'I know that I know.' Some people get angry at other people's views, because they regard their own views as facts. They follow their conviction as a matter of principle, which can lead to idiotic results. What do you do?

See through the generator of empty phrases

You will certainly have met him, the well-dressed generator of empty phrases. He has a broad smile, an impressive vocabulary, and he says... nothing. But since he sounds so smart, you don't dare ask him what he means. With his broad smile, he describes his company like this:

> "We concentrate on knowledge and professionalism. We can offer a number of exciting concepts within the design of new solutions to exceed the demands of our clients and ourselves."

That sounds great, you might think, without having a proper picture of what the generator of empty phrases is really offering. But words like 'exciting', 'knowledge' and 'professionalism' do sound fantastic. He develops this further:

> "We have a flexible client-oriented attitude and have client-adapted solutions with a high success rate. And everything is geared towards enabling and empowering the end-user."

A generator of empty phrases says precisely nothing. He uses sweeping, compelling words that you can easily take in. But he is never concrete. In the same way that the politician uses pretty words that a lot of people can take in. But they never actually say what their 'solidarity' or 'improved society' look like. Confront these people by saying, "That sounds lovely, but you will have to be more specific about what you mean by *improved Sweden*, so give me an example." If he answers, "Things will be better for you!" then you should simply reply, "Now you sound like a generator of empty phrases; the words sound nice but you aren't saying what it means in concrete terms."

See through the people who refer to an authority

There are those who try to strengthen their credibility by referring to an authority. 'XYZ thinks the same as me'. The implication, in their mind, is that it is therefore correct. In my rhetoric analyses, I usually call this *ethos reinforcement*.

Ethos reinforcement is good if it is based on the right foundations, but can be dangerous since it has an enormous effect on the listeners. We are all more or less programmed to worship authorities. Somebody might say, "I met XYZ and he said that blue is the ultimate colour." We nod in agreement. We're enchanted by the fact that this person actually met the great authority. It gets wrong when you rely on *who* said it, rather than thinking about *what* the person said, and worst of all without finding out *what grounds* there are for the statement. Even an authority can be wrong. So, my tip when somebody uses ethos reinforcement to convince you is to simply ask, "And how did XYZ (the authority) come to that conclusion? Please tell me more!" In that way, you will seem curious, when what you really want is to see through the argument. Someone who uses mudslinging rhetoric focuses on sinking the other person since he or she can't find sufficiently good arguments to sink the person's arguments.

Mudslinging rhetoric
(argumentum ad hominem)

If you want to know when the argumentation of the person you are listening to is extremely thin, then you should listen to what he says. If he starts out with a personal attack, that is a sign that he can't beat the person he is attacking. That is why he is not attacking what has been said – but the person who has said it. They attack real or imagined qualities in the person, but the attacks have nothing to do with the person's competence or views.

I was the victim of a lot of personal attacks when I was the rhetoric expert for *Aftonbladet* [an evening newspaper] during the 2010 election. This happened when people either didn't like me or the conclusions of my analysis.

"Why should I listen to what a 23-year-old says about politicians?"
"The rhetoric expert would fit in better in a bad porno film."
"She has been bribed by the red-green parties."
"She has been bribed by the Alliance."

Even though it is fun to hear that I looked as young as 23 years old, these kicks were rather low. They were kicking at me, not at what I said. So, when you hear someone attack a person, be curious and ask them, "Now I know what you think about her, but can you tell me more as to what you think about what she says?" If you don't get any answers, you know that the person is attacking because they lack any relevant counter-arguments.

The false dilemma (false dichotomy)

There are those who see things in black and white, heaven or hell, red or blue. For these people, it is very difficult to see that something could be relative, because their view of life only has two positions. In extreme cases, they have psychopathic elements and formulate sentences such as, 'Either you are for me, or against me. You choose!' And you yourself sit there wondering how you found yourself in this dilemma. The answer is simple – you are not in a fix. You have come across a 'black-or-white' person. And as soon as you realize that, the alternatives immediately become more than the ones presented by the manipulator. These people are everywhere and they find it easy to convince people of like mind. And others too – those with different views but who lack the ability to see through the manipulators, who cast out a false dilemma to get a decision that suits them better.

I worked with just such a person. Every week the managing director came to a new insight and at the same time mixed with new friends who understood the dilemma of his world. We who didn't? He looked down on us with pitying eyes and said, "You will understand one day." We were drawn to him, or rather to his naïve conviction. What made me suspicious was that he never realised just how often he changed his views. For him, the world was black or white. Those who didn't share his views got the sack, or he convinced them to leave their job with their tail between their legs. He threw out old insights, and those who had supported them. Towards the end, we employees dared to ask the question, "And what do you think about this?" and present three, four and sometimes five alternatives to the two that the MD had in mind. He simply couldn't understand how we thought. But thank God the alternatives will beat false dilemmas as soon as somebody dares to present them.

After the 9/11 attacks in New York, 'terrorism' and 'the light' became the two alternatives that George Bush thought that all of us should choose between. He turned to the world and read clear and loud these words from the teleprompter, "You are either with us, or with the terrorists."

At a single blow, the entire world had been involuntarily ensnared in a false dilemma that Bush had taken from – believe it or not – the Bible. In Matthew 12:30 Jesus is quoted saying those words: "Whoever is not with me is against me." Well suited to the Christian right-wing circles in the US, which cheered Bush. But they forgot another quote: "Thou shalt not kill." (Exodus, 20:13). Which brings us to another tendency among manipulators. Namely, selective information (focusing), something that we shall look at later.

As soon as you only have two alternatives, remember that in nine out of ten cases there will be other proposals that the manipulator has chosen to exclude. Either deliberately, or simply because the person sees the world in that way. He could be a psychopath, or quite involuntarily and innocently manipulative. The alternatives are many, but all you need to do is to be attentive when the dilemma presents itself.

It might also be that the alternatives that are presented fall outside the frame. A course participant once asked me, "Which rhetoric is most convincing, female or male?" I had to think for a moment because there was something wrong with that question. To start with, I see female and male as something biologically determined. There are, however, tendencies that women and men, respectively, *can* have, but that is not always the case. And the art of convincing people is not linked to gender. Rhetoric helps people to be credible. If a person is convincing, it is because he or she is so, not thanks to which sex they are. This is not a gender dilemma.

Not everybody who sees life in black and white does so consciously, nor do they all want to do harm to anybody. But they do often harm themselves and others on account of their attitude. Perhaps they see a more successful person and conclude that they themselves have been unsuccessful. I had some friends who vanished when my first book, *Domination Technique*, ended up on the bestsellers list and I was featured in the media. They didn't want to feel like they did, but every time they socialised with me they felt relatively unsuccessful. I have reacted the same way myself. At the gym I always felt how the layers of stomach fat wobbled with each step I took, even though I tried to hold my tummy in. One day I saw a woman bounce along down the corridor, with a perfect body and a ponytail that she flipped with her head in a disturbingly energetic way. With each step she took, her ponytail rocked. "Hello!" she chirped. I smiled back… and thought, 'I hate you.' But of course there were alternatives to, 'She is successful, so I am unsuccessful'. There was 'I shall be like that'. Then I too can bounce along the corridor with my bob of hair and my rings of fat rocking perfectly because I have taken a step away from the fetid swamp of comparison. There are more than two alternatives, so drop the dilemma!

The popularity argument - 'As everyone knows...' (argumentum ad populum)

Some people trick you into thinking that something is good or bad just because 'so many others' think that. They use popularity as a reason. And sure, if you are of a fairly democratic nature, then you should trust the majority. But that does not mean that the majority is always right. Don't refrain from examining the issue; instead you should ask what that good, or bad, popular vote is based on. The important thing is that the answer is not 'because so many others think so'. There must be other arguments. Popular views – ones that the majority of people have held – have changed over the ages. Once the Earth was flat, clever women were witches, etc. Today we laugh at (or cry over) how stupid people were back then. But the fact is that future generations are going to laugh or cry over how stupid we are today. Again, don't fall for the popularity argument, but examine which arguments they are built upon. So if the person says, "A lot of people think like me," you can answer, "A lot of people have been wrong before, so tell me what you're basing your statement on besides that."

Guilt by association

Sometimes the manipulator wants you to stop listening to a certain person because he or she can be associated with something negative. 'She has done stupid things, so she isn't credible'. Instead of *for or against* arguments, they use negative associations to steer other people's attitudes. This affected the SD when they took part in the parliamentary election in 2010. The media associated them with the White Power movement and other negative links. Was that successful? It depends on what they wanted to achieve, but for SD it was good. Their leader, Jimmie Åkesson, quite simply answered that it was unfortunate, but that no party in Sweden can completely liberate itself from racism or hidden racism. "That isn't unique to the Swedish Democrats," he said.

Yet the media continued along the same lines instead of confronting what SD said.

Of course one ought to know about a person's background to see if he lives as he preaches. There are those who want to teach others how to bring up children, but who themselves have insufferable children, and those who 'know' how to earn money, but never seem to have any themselves. It is a balancing act. And if you dig deeply enough, probably everybody has some skeleton or other in their wardrobe. What is important is that it can be linked to what the person is talking about; otherwise it is guilt by association.

You can parry with a question, "Yes, I did do what you claim, but what does that have to do with what we are talking about now?"

Focusing - selective information

This phenomenon means that a person gives you part of the picture, but not the whole thing. To focus, the people start by saying, "Let us begin with the big problem," but only take up the little one. Unwittingly you accept that this part takes more time because it was called 'big'. These people don't want you to get the whole picture. What you then can do is move the focus to other parts of the problem. And that is exactly what George Bush did. He justified his actions by focusing on a little part of the Bible, but excluded another part that says, "Thou shalt not kill." That is how people who focus can go on. They get you to sign a contract by focusing on certain bits and glossing over the others. See through the focusing person by probing what has been left in the dark.

Objective hiding places

As soon as people want to hide behind their actions and avoid taking responsibility for things being done, or not being done, they objectify the action. They diminish the person and make the action responsible. Hiding behind standard expressions – the same tired old clichés – means they can avoid taking responsibility. Your boss or your colleague may say, "It's being done" about something that actually doesn't look like it's going to be done. To see through this, it is important that you pull out the person behind it. Ask, "Who's doing it?" It is necessary to pull the people out from their objective hiding places.

'This will be studied…' – Who will study it, when, and how will they go about it?

'It's often said…' – Who says it, are they credible, and what precisely do they say?

'It isn't done like that…' – Is it just you who thinks it isn't done that way, or is that the general consensus?

Unwarranted alternatives

"I didn't think you were stingy," a colleague answered when I didn't share some private information.

"No," I replied, "You can go on thinking that. I am not stingy, I'm generous. What we're talking about now is something quite different. You think that I reveal everything, but in actual fact I have integrity."

When the manipulators don't get what they want, they will readily put incorrect labels on you – characterizations that are sometimes really quite bizarre. It might be that you don't want to help somebody with some work task.

"RIGHT, so you think I'm lazy! I knew it!" – a weird approach in which the manipulator links to your statement or action. A lot of people fall for this, as far-fetched as it may seem. This can happen in relationships too:

"Darling, can you make me some food?"

"No, I'm too tired."

Long, silent pause.

"Is that OK?"

"Of course it isn't. You don't give a damn about me!"

The manipulator links unwarranted conclusions to your actions. If I had been a psychologist, I would have said, "Try to understand the manipulator's mind and what it says." But, since I am a rhetorician, I don't dig into people's minds but into their expressions. If you want to be diplomatic, you can ask, "What do you mean by that?" If you want to make a point and set a limit, say, "Those are your words, not mine. Now you have created something that I do not support and I am not going to step into a discussion where I have unwarranted labels hung on me." And, as in all situations, say it in your own words – not mine.

Question traps

'Do you want €5,000?'

Question traps are common with salesmen. It is a way to hook us – on the phone, or on the street – a bit longer that we had intended. When I was walking along Drottninggatan in Stockholm I saw, 20 metres away, how a woman had already started her selling by arousing good will – she admittedly had her hands behind her back, but she nevertheless smiled innocently at me. I smiled back and looked down at the ground and kept on walking. I glanced up discreetly to see if she was still looking at me – perhaps we even knew each other – and *oops*, she was still looking at me and smiling. Guilty feelings built up inside me. When I was five metres from her, she stretched out her hand holding a piece of paper. I walked towards the piece of paper, smiled and heard her say in a jolly tone, "Do you want €5,000?" I gave a start. My smile vanished. In those few seconds she had managed to give me a bad conscience, and I felt a bit stupid for answering, "No." Who doesn't want €5,000? She set a trap and asked a question that is intended only to generate the answer 'Yes'. But that means we must stay there with the salesman. So a better answer would have been, "I certainly would, but in my own way! Goodbye!"

Or take the telemarketer who phones you and says in a jolly tone, "Hello Elaine!" It's embarrassing for me not to recognise the voice saying my name. It builds up a bad conscience. "Hello!" is how we answer. "Am I disturbing you?" is the second polite phrase and now, for God's sake, you should never say 'no' because then you are hooked. Say instead, "That depends; if you are a salesman, then you are disturbing me." That has helped me to shake off all the telemarketers who try to trick us into thinking that we must listen to them. Sometimes I have practised rapport and started to offer my own instructional work to the salesman: "Great that you phoned. Now we can talk about rhetoric and how you can become a better salesman. It only costs..." They usually end the call very quickly. You can try that too; you can try to sell them anything at all!

They stand on the sidewalk with pictures of children in tears, and they themselves smile hopefully in a way that says, 'I believe you are a good person, so stop and give the children some money'. We get a bad conscience. They fire off guilt-trip phrases like, 'Do you want to help the starving children in...' We cut them off with a routine 'no' and walk on – with a bad conscience. Pick up the salesman's phrase and say instead, "YES, I do want to help the children in MY way! Goodbye!" You grasp the question, weave it into your answer, and go on your way.

Euphemisms

'You have a opportunity to look for a new job' = you are sacked.
'I'm going to let you move on' = you are sacked.
'You have the opportunity to do this' = work overtime.
'It isn't you, it's me' = you are dumped.
'I am not ready to be with you just now' = you are dumped.

As soon as somebody comes at you with these nice-sounding euphemisms there is always something hidden behind them. You can feel it in your gut, or you notice it when you work overtime as a result of the 'offer' you got from the boss. So it is important to ask yourself what is hidden behind those well-turned phrases.

When politicians offer tax reductions, you should always ask, 'How will that be paid for?' When you are offered free dental treatment you can ask the same thing: 'How will that be paid for?' All nice-sounding formulations have something hidden behind them if they are euphemistic. If you are suspicious then you should ask critical follow-up questions. 'And what is this going to mean?' or 'What is this going to cost me?' Dig out anything uncomfortable in those pleasant sounding phrases and do so by asking pertinent questions that tempt the manipulator to answer.

Disguise of uncomfortable questions (Abstraction)

Imagine you are standing in a sweet shop. Your brain is bombarded with signal colours and the sweet smells make your mouth water. You leave the shop with a green bag filled with sugary treats. You pop the first one into your mouth – a sugary dummy. Delightfully red and green, colours that attract your attention. But what does the sweet consist of? Citric acids, some artificial colours and something called gelatin. Sure, gelatin sounds harmless enough. The innocent dummy wouldn't have looked so tasty without its colours and the euphemism gelatin. But what does it mean? If you look it up online you will find another word for gelatin – *collagen*. And you'll learn the following: 'Collagen is mainly found in fibrous tissues such as tendons, ligaments and skin... cartilage, bones, blood vessels...' Just add a bit of colour and citric acids and you get – (drumroll!) – your sugary dummy.

Abstractions are extremely common. The sender used other words to avoid bringing up uncomfortable information and questions. A typical place where such euphemistic wording is used is on food packaging. How many words do you understand on those lists of ingredients? And how much would they have sold if it had said: 'Bones, skin, tendons, blood-vessel walls, a bit of sweetener and artificial colours'? This is called abstraction. It is when the sender hides truths that are uncomfortable by leaving out concrete details. The truth becomes less evident, and the result is incomprehensible language constructs instead of tangible facts. This is a way to make a controversial question less risky – by using a bureaucratic formulation. Let me give an example.

In the Swedish TV interview with Prime Minister Reinfeldt in 2010, he had to deal with uncomfortable questions about people on long-term sick leave and those who were no longer covered by national insurance. He found it difficult to answer the questions that he got about specific people, for example Carina, who had used up all her insurance benefits and was no longer covered. Reinfeldt didn't devote any time to saying he could sympathize with her situation, nor did he name her. Instead he adopted a helicopter perspective to create distance, and called the group of people on sick leave 'ill-health figures' – he characterized them as statistical numbers. That's one way to disguise the problem. Make it more abstract and even switch the focus away from the individuals on sick leave. Try to imagine what an 'ill-health figure' looks like. There is no obvious image; perhaps you will only see the words 'ill-health figure'. And that was exactly what Reinfeldt wanted, since it was an uncomfortable question for him. But the fact is that someone might be one among group of many, but they are not just a figure. They are a thinking, feeling, flesh and blood person.. If the voters see through this, Reinfeldt risks being seen as an unfeeling person, a leader with a lot of brain (logos) but little heart (pathos).

In the USA, where rhetoric is well established, politicians realise what they risk if they avoid dealing with voters' questions. The combination of brain, heart and personality (ethos) must always be there in a leader. That is why the political parties and power brokers make such an effort to find a candidate who didn't necessarily begin their political career in their youth, but who has the competence and leadership qualities that the people want to see. When someone like Carina, who has lost her insurance coverage, asks a question, she is focused upon. Abstraction and diffuse concepts don't have a place here. Trot them out on the campaign trail and you could lose an election.

During the 2008 US presidential campaign, Samuel Joseph Wurzelbacher (Joe the Plumber) received considerable attention when he questioned Barack Obama's tax policy. Obama's Republican opponent, John McCain, seized the opportunity, turning towards the TV cameras with a pointing finger and addressed Joe: "I want you, Joe, to know that…" Perhaps that seems rather too 'American', but it is effective. People knew that McCain wasn't just speaking to Joe but to all the others who had the same question. Joe became, one could say, a part that could represent the whole (*synecdoche*).

Reinfeldt should simply have mentioned Carina's situation before moving on to the whole. How then do you deal with a person who makes use of an abstraction? Well, by asking logically sequential questions so that the person is forced to come out from behind their disguise.

Reinfeldt: "We have a large ill-health figure in Sweden."
Critical listener: "What do you mean by ill-health figures?"
Reinfeldt: "The number with ill health."
Critical listener: "And what do you mean by number with ill health?"
Reinfeldt: "Well that is self-evident."
Critical listener: "Perhaps, but tell us what you mean so that everyone will understand."
Reinfeldt: "The number of people who are on sick leave and can't work."
Critical listener: "OK, the number of *people* who are on sick leave."

The point is that you should ask questions until the sender has formulated their answer in a way that allows everyone to understand and *see* the problem. It isn't easy for your brain to see something as abstract as an 'ill-health figure', but it can easily see pictures of people on sick leave. There is a reason why certain people make use of abstraction. The sender does not want you to see the awkward message, because then you will be moved by it.

A story that greatly moved me also showed how incredibly inhuman an abstraction can be. A Norwegian woman found out that her struggle against cancer was over in a decidedly inconsiderate way. The doctor came in and said, "Well, Ida, we're going to move you to the palliative care ward at Ullevål Hospital, and they will take over responsibility." Ida had to Google the word palliative to find out what it meant. Since the doctor had chosen abstraction rather than concrete information, she received her death sentence after a Google search. 'Palliative care is a form of treatment that focuses more on reducing and alleviating symptoms than on finding a cure.' (Reported in *Aftonbladet*).

There are many ways of giving unpleasant information nicely, but abstraction is not one of them.

How to reveal values

You can reveal values in your choice of words. There is a great difference if your partner says, 'I'm going to the house' instead of 'I'm going home'. You can have cause for worry if he calls your home 'the house'. I once asked a researcher, "Couldn't you use words and expressions that people understand, and reduce the use of academic terminology?"

"I wouldn't lower myself to that level," he answered, revealing his fundamental dislike for language that people could actually understand.

My response: I thought that one raised oneself by achieving understanding. If someone says 'raise' or 'lower' about various actions, they are revealing how they value these actions.

"Where is Hannes?"

"He'll probably soon crawl in..."

The person doesn't like Hannes and compares him to something lowly that crawls.

When Liberal Party leader Jan Björklund got angry at the programme hosts on TV4, he said, "You are smearing me with prejudices that I don't have." The word 'smear' showed clearly what he thought about the questions he was being asked. "The Muslims are breeding." The word 'breed' and 'they are increasing' were expressions used by SD supporters during the 2010 election campaign to dehumanise Muslims. When I interviewed party leader Jimmie Åkesson afterwards, he distanced himself from that choice of words.

People have children, and animals breed. One can also say that vermin breed. But you don't go to your pregnant friend and say, 'Well, I see you are breeding.' If you refer to their family, you wouldn't say, 'They are increasing'. Think about it – you wouldn't say about rats in the underground, 'They've had babies.'

If you want to plant a positive feeling, the formulation is important. 'I'm becoming less suspicious' could be formulated as, 'My confidence is greater'. Those are two formulations that mean the same thing. But the first reveals a negative standpoint and attitude. 'I am less fat' could be formulated as, 'I'm slimmer'. 'You aren't as bad' could become, 'You're better'. And finally, 'We can't pay for this' instead of 'We can't invest in this' reveals whether the potential buyer sees a purchase as wasted money or a wise investment. When you enter a shop, the manufacturers have chosen which values are going to be aroused when you see that bar of chocolate. It is sitting there on the shelf and looking at you. It is especially inviting since it says that it is all of '80% fat free'! Wow, one might think. But that figure means of course that the rest of the bar is 20% pure fat. But we don't think about that, since the manufacturer doesn't emphasize it. Remember that all offers have a reverse side.

When you feel that something is suspicious, remember this:

The generator of empty phrases – he talks eloquently about nothing.

Reference to an authority – he wants you to think like he does just because some higher authority does so.

The mudslinger – attacks the person instead of attacking what the person does or says.

The dilemma person – wants to fool you into choosing between two alternatives that he has chosen.

The 'everyone knows that's the case' person – tries to get you to think something by referring to how many others think it.

The focus person – steers your attention towards one part so that you miss the other parts.

'Hiding place for the perpetrators' – this is when somebody wants to hide who the people are, by using objective formulations such as 'it is done' or 'it has happened'. On occasion he will want you to believe that things happen, by using the formulation, 'It is being examined'. Fish out the people who are said to be doing it, and ask how, in precise terms.

The 'Oh so you are one of those' people – this is the type who links your actions to an unwarranted conclusion.

Question traps – beware of answering yes or no to this person, it is just a strategy to get you closer to his intentions with the question.

The embellisher – he reformulates unpleasant things. Overtime becomes 'chance to work', getting the sack becomes 'letting you move on'. He wraps up everything – tasks, overtime and insults – in elaborate formulations.

The abstractor – makes uncomfortable truths abstract.

You could write a whole book about rhetorical pitfalls – one that I can recommend is *Skeptikerskolan* (School for Sceptics).

Chapter

The influence
of music and
the internet
on rhetoric

The influence of music

When you read this chapter, I want you to do something. Listen to a song that gets to your heart – one that takes you on a journey that leads directly to good memories. And think about the feelings and memories that the song arouses.

Every day we are awash in – and influenced by – music. Film directors steer our emotions with the help of tones. When you look at a film and suddenly become emotionally moved, you can't be entirely certain whether it was the music or what you saw that gave you that feeling. It can, of course, be a combination of the two, but the music strengthens the impressions. Companies use music strategically, to get you to act in a certain way. If you go into a shop with high-tempo music, it is probably a low-price establishment where they want you to do your shopping quickly and leave. Test this by strolling around particularly slowly in a shop where they're playing techno and you will notice that it requires some effort. In the same way, a meeting can be more or less successful depending on the background music. You can use music strategically to create a mood that convinces the listener. It can create a feeling that you want to achieve and help lighten conversations. It is a powerful tool if you use it correctly.

Silence can also be effective, and sometimes make things uncomfortable. Shop-owners prefer not to have silent premises. Think about it – you and a silent salesperson in a totally silent shop. Background music eases the negative vibes. And it can also increase turnover in a shop. The newspaper *Servicehandlaren* describes an English wine shop that had a shelf with both French and German wines. When they played French music, they sold five French bottles for every German one. If they played German music they sold two German bottles for each French one. The choice of music alone steered the buying pattern. When the shop asked their customers about it, they reported not even realising they'd heard music. Another example deals with the sale of eggs in a supermarket. Sales increased dramatically when they played the sound of cackling hens! Music in shops is not a new phenom-enon. In the 1980s, Domus [Swedish cooperative department stores] carried out an experiment where they played music every second day in their stores. It turned out that turnover increased by 3.6% on the days when they played music.

Some people believe that music can have an effect on physical treatments. The neurologist Oliver Sacks, who wrote the book *Musicophilia*, was of the opinion that music can have incredible effects on people with neurological conditions such as Parkin-son's, dementia, stroke and aphasia. Music seems to have a unique ability to tap into inner abilities that people had lost. Part of the explanation for this is that the various components of music, such as rhythm, timbre and beat, affect different parts of the brain. Since music triggers emotional as well as cognitive, autonomic and motor functions, it stimulates many parts of the brain.

Music producer Björn Melander says this: 'The body and mind tend to copy what we experience with our ears. If we surround ourselves with sound sceneries that have a lower tempo, and are experienced as being more harmonious, we often become more harmonious ourselves.' Meditative music often lacks a distinct pulse and melody. This is so that it will stimulate the analytical right side of the brain. In summary, one could say that traditional relaxation music follows the heart's pulse at rest, while inspiring, uplifting music has more tempo and melody. Test this by going for a run to meditative music. You will soon notice that it wasn't very successful. Just as bad is trying to relax and have a calm con-versation in a café that plays frenetic techno music. So how can one use music strategically?

When I wrote my second book, *Du är din generation* (You are Your Generation), I wanted to get as much information as possi-ble about people born in the 1930s, and all the generations up to those born in the 1980s. I decided to create focus groups where people of a particular generation got to meet. My purpose was to find common denominators and take them back to the time when they grew up. They filled in a web questionnaire before they came to the meetings. The questions included, 'What music did you listen to?' and 'What did you listen to on radio and TV?' It wasn't easy for me to take the 1940s generation back to a time that I myself had never experienced, but music helped me along the way. The people in the focus groups did not know each other, but their faces took on a nostalgic expression when they heard the intro jingle to the radio programme they'd heard on Saturdays during their childhood years:

'G'morning, g'morning! Hear the birds sing away: g'morning, g'morning, to youuuu.'

When they heard this old jingle for the first time in many decades, their hearts were moved. The music transported them back to their childhood years. What first hit them was a sense of nostalgia. The music aroused memories and facilitated my interview work. It became a powerful instrument to place the listener in the time, place and feeling I wanted. What feeling do you want to give your listeners?

> "I don't know if it is our working partner or the music he has in the background when I go there. He says, anyhow, that he likes Bollywood music. I am from India, not especially fond of Bollywood music. But the fact that he even listens to and plays my country's music makes me in some way feel at home every time we see each other." – Shari, a participant on one of my rhetoric courses

Of course it can be like that. When you visit somebody's home for the first time and he plays music that is familiar to you, you feel at home. For shops that want to appeal to the affluent baby-boomer generation and put them in a particularly good mood, the Rolling Stones or Beatles could be a good alternative. You can fill a room with 1960s feelings by choosing music from that time.

Speaking of shops, a participant on one of my rhetoric courses started to use music strategically after our session together. She worked in a clothes shop in Stockholm and had received a double delivery of polka-dot dresses in a classic 1950s style. She played Elvis and other music typical of the period. When people stepped into the shop and heard the music, their mental image of the period matched the wares in the shop. The dresses sold out. She was completely convinced that it was the strategic choice of music that helped her to sell every last dress. Don't be surprised if you, as a consumer, fall into the same trap. The shop plays hard rock and suddenly you find yourself buying the bag with studs, even though you don't even like the music.

Music can also be treacherous. For a while I was a member of an Evangelical church congregation. We sat in the middle of the church and listened to one of the pastors up on stage. He was a charismatic speaker. The pastor read some well-chosen chapters from the Bible, and for us who listened they represented facts. He told of God's love for man, how he gave us his only son, who like a sacrificial lamb took on the burden of all our sins and died for us. We were filled with gratitude. Then he wanted to reach our emotions and link the story to our day-to-day lives. Suddenly the pianist started to play sad music, accompanying the pastor as he held his appeal for the collection, where the congregation gives money. At the same time that the music gripped our hearts, we gripped our wallets and handed over our cash. And it was, as the pastor had said, 'For Jesus'. Music can become manipulative if it comes into the wrong hands. So it is important to listen sharply when you're in a meeting where the music sounds nice, but the message is so-so. There's always a risk that the music rings through louder than the message simply because you connect it so strongly with something nice.

Sometimes the opposite can apply. At times the message, or event, is louder than the music. Say that you are sitting with your partner and you favourite song is playing. Beautiful memories wash over you. Aromas, pictures and delightful feelings. Suddenly your partner utters the classic words that bring such magical moments to a resounding end: "We must talk." 'No,' you think. One after another, your memories associated with the song are wiped away. Instead, new tragic pictures push their way in and remind you that you were dumped to this song. Your bad gut feeling is encapsulated in the song. Sorrow, the setting, your boyfriend's facial expression. He has ruined that lovely song so that you will probably never be able to listen to it again.

I lecture on average four or five times a week. The audience is generally quite large and needs to take their seats relatively quickly if we're to begin on time. I often use tempo music to get them to move quicker, and it works. If, however, I am holding a rhetoric course with twelve visibly nervous participants, I usually play calm music. Not meditative – I don't want them to think they've come to the wrong course – but something that slows down their pulse. Just think if hospitals had music in their waiting rooms. That would probably result in fewer irritated patients. Waiting music on telephones, which plays when you're put on hold, works well too. It has been shown that people are willing to wait longer when they hear music while they are waiting.

Which music has the greatest effect? Is there any particular song that always works? No, what affects us all similarly is the rhythm. But the other emotions that are aroused are different. Find out which music your listeners are influenced by. According to Ingrid Hammarlund, music therapist and teacher at the Royal College of Music, researchers today agree that the music that is most effective, medically and psychologically, is that which you choose yourself. Let your listener choose.

Magical, transporting films often manage to plant emotions without showing them. We 'hear' the feelings, but don't see them, or read them with words.

One film in which the director used music strategically is *Vicky Christina Barcelona* (2008) by Woody Allen. Allen succeeds in planting a feeling with some guitar notes that turn up on various occasions in the film. Vicky, a character who is soon to be married, is passionate about Spanish guitar music. A stranger she falls in love with takes her with him to a guitar concert. Further on in the film, she is sitting talking with her future husband and their mutual friends. For viewers, Vicky seems to be taking part in the conversation, but then the same guitar notes are played and we know she's thinking about the stranger she has fallen in love with. Without a word, the director conveys what he wants us to feel and understand.

Sophie Zelmani's song *Always You* takes me directly back to 1996 and my cousin Wendy's terrace. We were two teenagers with goals in life. Our primary interest was boys and getting good grades at school. I sat on the floor while Wendy hummed to the song in her hammock. The smell of food seeped from the kitchen and the birch trees had just started to come into leaf. I was worried that the wasps would attack me, and my first boyfriend, Jacob, thought my tummy was too large. The song encapsulated those feelings and every time I hear it I think back to those memories. It is a cosy feeling that I smile at today. Tiny problems were big, and life was a mystery.

What do you want to say? What feeling do you want to convey? Use music strategically to arouse the right feelings in the person you are going to meet. Think about the tempo in the music, but also the age, background and musical taste of the listener.

Internet rhetoric - getting people to 'listen' on the internet

How many web pages have you seen? That question is, of course, impossible to answer, and if I ask you to list the ones that have really made an impression it would be even harder. The art of communicating has come quite a lot further IRL – in real life – than it has done on the web, and the reason is quite simply that the internet hasn't been around so very long.

I am certain that you with your modern rhetorical tools can even be interesting out there on the worldwide web.

Let it take time - but not on the web

When I commissioned a company to create the rhetoric bureau's website, I wanted it to be really something. "It should not only knock out all other rhetoric sites, but all websites," I said to them in their office.

The result was a grand website – and an equally grand invoice. But, well, I was pretty cocky! But there was a downside – nobody found it. Or could be bothered.

If the time it takes to download your web pages feels like a trip back to the '90s, with dial-up connectivity and crackling modems, then I can promise you that visitors are not going to stay or return. Nobody could be bothered to wait for the rhetoric bureau's super-duper flash site to download. Our delightful home page took such a long time that I was forced to re-think it and do something much simpler.

Remember that the superior technical features don't determine whether a visitor stays on your site. The old saying that 'less is more' is still relevant, and on the internet 'fast is king'. But, not surprisingly, the most important question the visitor has is: 'What's in it for me?'

From three minutes to one click!

If you want to catch someone's attention on the web, the same rules apply as those beyond the computer's keyboard. The difference is that if something in the real world takes three minutes, that time is reduced on the web to a single click. Everything goes so very much quicker, while the possibilities for reaching out to so many are enormous.

Now, instead, the shell is the web site's graphic profile, structure and tone – the first page that turns up, which the visitor meets with. And remember that apart from your business idea, that first encounter ought to arouse three feelings: goodwill, curiosity and credibility. There are different ways of doing this, but it is important that the picture that greets a visitor doesn't feel too abstract. The site should feel credible, nice and relevant. As a visitor one should feel:

- This seems to be a nice gang (goodwill)
- I fathom exactly what I can get from them (curiosity)
- They really know their stuff (credibility)

What does your company's website look like? Have a look and write down the first three things that strike you. If it is boring, messy and irrelevant, then your social media team has a lot to work with.

The next step is to 'dress' the site. You should create a structure with various sub-pages that are suitable for what you want to achieve. Do you want to create closeness? If so, it is good if the visitor can see who works in the company. On the *Contact Us* page there should be photos of the actual people who work there, not a gaggle of models from a photo agency. Stick to what is genuine – people will see through everything else.

The site must be easy to navigate! Clear away any complicated instructions. Don't try to say everything or describe your entire knowledge bank in the text – just deal with what is immediately relevant for the visitor, what you want him or her to know *quickly.*

Study other websites

When I looked for a name for my rhetoric bureau, I looked around to see what my competitors had called theirs and noticed that there were plenty of company names that referred to ancient Greece. I wanted to stick out and had written a list of what I thought my company radiated: a modern, reliable and genuinely nice gang.

The name was chosen – Snacka Snyggt [an English equivalent might be the Gift of the Gab] – the colour scale was a harmonious blue and in a photo you can see our team of jolly consultants.

Many of our clients hadn't heard of us before, but say that they found us on the internet. And several say that it was the stark contrast with the other rhetoric services that attracted them. One could say that the website went from being pompous, expensive and anonymous to being easy to find, welcoming and attractive. So my point is: don't be afraid to stick out! And don't just copy and paste. Make something of your own that's not just good – make it the best in the genre.

Social media

I have a blog, am on Facebook and I post tweets. If you want to check what people say about you, the social media provide excellent feedback at virtually no cost, other than a bit of time. There is a golden rule for making maximum use of these tools, and it is: make your tweets, Facebook updates and blog entries attractive for others.

Facebook

Is the great, universal meeting place of Facebook relevant for your company or for you as a private person? You can choose to leverage it as a marketing channel or a social tool.

I chose marketing when the social stress from people I don't even know became too great. You can't interact with too many people and I got a bad conscience when I didn't answer messages. Instead I turned my Facebook page into a company page, a fan page. That is one-way communication and an excellent marketing channel. To keep up with friends and family, I pick up the phone, just like in the good old days.

Your trademark on the internet says quite a lot about you. Are you a person who describes everything or just posts interesting updates? Pay attention to how you update your status with things that can be interesting for your friends. By doing so, they will all see a pattern and know that it is worth following you.

Be generous with humour, interesting meeting opportunities, good offers, a thoughtful reflection. Let it be a glorious mix, but stick to the basic rule: everybody should get something from it. Your Facebook page can in that way be a good starting page for others.

Twitter

This is a relatively new medium for me, but I have about 7,000 followers and try to give them mini-versions of my blog posts. It is a good way to generate traffic to the blog. There are some things I think about that you can also bear in mind:

- All tweets should give something. To just tweet that you are 'eating cake' is not an option – it gives nothing
- I try to answer all tweets. Media-rhetoric expert Paul Ronge, who at the moment has 6,000 followers, answers everybody on Twitter. "You can always give them a smiley," says Paul
- Always stick to a pleasant tone
- Never tweet in the heat of the moment
- If you don't want to give yourself a profile on Twitter, but still 'have a presence', create an account so that everyone can see you

Blog rhetoric

When I decided that this was going to be a modern book about rhetoric, I realised I needed a little help. I contacted one of the blog mothers, Isabella Löwengrip – known as Blondinbella. When I followed her advice, the number of visitors to my blog increased from 300 a week to 130,000, which I have at the time of writing this. But the *number* of readers shouldn't be the goal, rather it is a question of attracting the *right* readers.

Exactly like in a personal meeting, the first few seconds – when the reader enters your blog – are decisive. It is then and there that you're 'going to hook her or him,' says Isabella.

"The readers should be able to see who you are, they should be able to describe the blog author. On the first page, you should visually show what your blog is about. If there are several posts on the first page and the reader starts to read them, it is important that the posts differ in content. Then the blog is interesting."

Vary text and images. It is also important that you, as the sender, are clear. The reader should be able to formulate a distinct picture of who you are and what your blog is about from your first four posts.

My blog, Elaine Eksvärd, stands on four feet: everyday rhetoric, training, thoughts about life and political rhetoric.

If you are going to have a blog where you mix personal and professional, you need a great capacity for looking at yourself from outside – and, since it is about you and your interests, you need to be a bit self-centred too.

Share those little details with your readers

The people who read your blog are not interested in a long stream of words, or they would have read a book. So if you want a lot of readers, and want them to return, write short pithy posts with amusing details. If your blog is in a special niche, and you want to attract the right target group, then do it like Paul Ronge – don't bother with everyday life, but keep it professional and interesting.

When you share the little details about your company, the blog readers will get a feel for those who work there. You can strategically lift up the firm's sharpest pen, who can paint a colourful blend of professional life and amusing details. In that way you will create 'personalities' to front your site, interesting people who become the company's face on the web.

Forget difficult language

Don't work to create prestige, but for closeness to your readers. If you use language that the readers don't understand, they will go to another blog. Avoid bureaucratic language and posh or fancy words if you want to reach out to the masses. Nobody wants to feel stupid, and it is easy to find yourself using a language that is too high-flown. And you'll lose that important feeling you wanted to arouse – good will.

If you are senior partner in a law firm and are thinking of blogging, but are afraid that people might not take you seriously, there is no reason not to start. "Get going!" says Isabella. "You can have a blog where you answer lightweight questions in a simple way about things like the legal aspects of living together without being married, and what the law says." If in your profession you use bureaucratic language with a lot of arcane, insiders' concepts, take on the challenge of simplifying it on your blog to make it accessible and attractive for the readers.

Study others - but do your own thing

"You can't just write about today's outfit, politics or what you you've just bought. That won't work. You must find your own niche. Sure, you might love fashion, but in that case you must concentrate on a particular type of style. Find something new. The name of the blog should be linked to your niche," says Isabella.

I felt that a rhetoric blog sounded really unsexy. But I could learn from the blog queens and make it more amusing. So I chose to give my blog a business angle. That is a permanent post I have almost every day since clothes communicate. In your branch, there will certainly be an idea behind the clothes and the norm. Tell your customers about it, they are more curious than you think.

"Think about more quantity. Be brief. I write between three and eight posts a day. If you are a company, then fine, it's OK to do two a week. But what is important is that something happens on your blog page," Isabella maintains, and she is after all one of the biggest bloggers in Sweden. So if you want to really start racking up your number of visitors, then *three to eight* is a tried-and-true formula.

Ignore nasty comments and private questions

If you don't respond to the haters, then they lose. They only want to steal your time and attention. Answering them simply gives them more energy. "Bear in mind that you only have 100% energy each day. How many per cent are those nasty people actually worth? Don't waste even one single per cent on them," says Isabella, giving me a meaningful look. "When it comes to private questions, you just ignore them. For my blog I write: *Personal but not private.*"

Checklist for successful internet rhetoric

- Fast is king – the less high-tech, the less patience is needed.
- Hook the reader at their first look at your homepage.
- As a rule of thumb, try to arouse good will, curiosity and credibility on the first page.
- Simple is brilliant – make the page easy to navigate.
- Make it attractive for others.
- Don't work with web specialists who talk unintelligibly; use simple language.
- Study other web pages.
- Do something new and individual.
- Write regularly so that the page is alive and creates traffic.
- Ignore nasty comments.

Chapter

9

Presentation techniques where you are the vehicle, not your slides

Did you know that a lot of people come to a halt on their career ladder and refuse to climb further because the next level means doing presentations in front of others? Let's not let that happen to you. Don't say no to opportunity and growth because you're afraid. Instead, you can become a devil at doing presentations. I shall teach you what to do and what you should avoid.

Some people pay companies to produce slide shows, using applications like PowerPoint. A 30-minute presentation might contain 99 slides. But with such a monstrous deck of slides you torpedo what it's all supposed to be about. The idea, after all, is to present a handful of points that the audience shouldn't miss.

And if you look at the word 'PowerPoint' you will notice it is singular – the original idea, in other words, was that you should present one point, not ninety-nine. There is nothing basically wrong with the tool; what is wrong is how people use it. Today it seems that presenters are using a karaoke machine, since they stand with their backs to the audience and read word-for-word from what is on the screen. It is your stories, not your slide show, that catch the listener's attention.

PowerPoint can be extremely effective in giving people an overview of what you are talking about. But there are some extremely good alternatives that you can use. After all, presentation technique is so much more than a bunch of slides. And the goal is to get people to listen to your presentation. So, let's take it step-by-step.

The room - mental as well as actual

Regardless of where the presentation takes place, don't forget to have your mental rhetorical place with you. When you stand in front of your listeners, you choose your favourite public – best friend, grandmother, wife. And you should do your presentation as if you were on that sofa, in that bar or sitting at that kitchen table. Many people lose themselves in presentation contexts and become nothing more than their professional sides – that is not going to happen to you. You shall have your best rhetorical version of yourself in a firm grip and the words should flow like running water.

You should 'own' the room where the presentation is being made. Nervousness will decrease considerably if you arrive there 30 minutes before all the others. Then you won't enter an unknown room filled with strangers; instead you will have some familiarity with the setting and those who listen will be guests in 'your room'. Walk around the room before your presentation and pretend that your best friend is sitting there. Test the technical equipment, and test talking through your introduction.

Beforehand, it can be helpful if you can get a photograph of the place where you will be making your presentation. To use the place in a meaningful way will improve the content of your presentation. It will be extremely attractive and entertaining for the listener.

The Lincoln Memorial became symbolic for Martin Luther King, giving that much more meaning to his classic 'I Have a Dream' speech, while also giving new and different meaning to that already historic place. He started his speech the same way that Abraham Lincoln had spoken the words, 'Four score and seven years ago', while he stood in front of the statue of Lincoln. The place helped reinforce King's confidence. Should you point to the nearest statue to enhance your presentation and your credibility? You don't need to do that, but you can if you want and if it is of value for your presentation. But make use of the room and see how you can weave it into your speech. If you have a metaphor about a window, you can point to one at the same time. Or get the audience to imagine the room somewhere else. Use your imagination, but above all use the room so that it benefits your presentation. If it is a bad room, you can tailor your introduction to say, 'This room is a bit shabby, but I promise that its contents are going to be of great value to you, so we can surely make allowances!'

The place is important. You need to know the conditions you are going to be and what contact you will be able to have with your audience. If it has a large stage, you need to plan the presentation so that you can walk back and forth, and everyone will feel seen. A little room, on the other hand, demands limited body language but lively facial expressions.

At university I had a classroom that faced an inner yard where people often stood talking, and without their knowing it they became props in part of the course that dealt with conversation techniques and body language. We stood there glued to the window, studying the body language of the people who went past. The classroom served as a rhetoric laboratory where people in the yard became unwary, but much appreciated, lab mice.

The presentation starts as soon as the listeners enter the room

When audience members start entering the space where you're going to make your presentation, it is important that you 'see' them. It is a bit like in a shop where the sales assistant gives you a welcoming and friendly look. You should do the same; from the very second that they step into the room, they will begin forming an impression of you. This is when the halo-effect kicks in. Create good will by looking people in the eye. That allows you to create a micro-relationship with each and every person, and you will feel less nervous.

There will be occasions when the technical equipment might cause problems or when you are not as well prepared as you would have liked. But you must nevertheless convey calm and happiness. You might have been to a presentation where the stressed speaker has not looked you in the eye when you entered the room, but instead has looked angry and been swearing at their non-functioning equipment. Alright, one might sympathize, but you won't be overly interested in the presentation. If the technology doesn't work, always have a Plan B, and unless it's glaringly obvious never let the public know that there is a problem. Say something like this instead: "Slide presentations are usually so boring anyway, so doing it this way is going to be even better." Then people will actually be pleased that the boring technology went wrong.

Frame in what you are going to talk about

When your listeners are seated, for them it is roughly like taking their seats at a restaurant. As a restaurant guest you will want to know what there is to eat, and to get that overview you will be given a menu. In the context of a presentation, that overview is just as important, but you should give it in the form of an agenda and a schedule. As we touched on earlier in this book, you should let people know when there will be breaks, how long you are going to speak for and, of course, what you are going to talk about. If you show *what* you are going to talk about in the form of bulleted points, that will help make every point interesting for your audience. They shouldn't be longing for the breaks but for what you are going to talk about. You'll know whether you have succeeded by asking them a special question after you've provided the agenda: "Does that sound interesting?" If they nod and answer yes, then you know. But bear in mind that if it is an introverted group, then you shouldn't expect a gushing 'hallelujah' response. And if there is no response at all, then say, "Okay, then we'll get going!"

A failure of a presentation, and the opposite of giving people a feeling of control and knowing what's coming, starts like this:

"First of all, I am going to teach you how to turn prejudices into advantages."

'Interesting,' thinks the listener.

"Secondly, I'll tell you how to use your clothes strategically."

'Great, that's just what I need. I wonder what the last point will be?'

"And third, I shall teach you to use your voice in such a way that other people listen."

'Sounds good too,' thinks the listener, nodding in satisfaction at having been given a summary of what the presentation is going to be about.

"Fourthly…"

'What? How many points is he going to cover?'

"The fifth item…"

'Is this a presentation about how many points he can cram in?'

"The sixth item…"
'???'

You can deal with as many points as you want. But in that case say how many at the beginning so the listener feels that he has control. Otherwise attention will start to fade at point four. Instead, say quite simply, "I am going to deal with four points and they are…" The structure of the presentation is those four points, which you will expand upon. And you end by saying, "Now you have heard about the four points I promised to cover." A psychologically sound method. You also tie things up nicely by beginning and ending in the same way.

Many films are built up following the same pattern. The musical score and certain images are identical in the beginning and at the end.

The film *Forrest Gump* starts with a scene where a feather hovers about streets, town squares and past people. When the same feather turns up at the end, we viewers know that the film has finished. It is a simple trick and gives us a pleasant feeling of foresight and control. Let your audience feel that they have control during your presentations and they will like you much more than the speaker who takes them on a point-marathon, listing point after point. And believe me, a lot of people use that never-ending-points style!

Start with a relevant story

If the listeners are going to stop looking at your clothes and instead try to work out who you are (which you want them to do as quickly as possible) you can begin with a story that leads them straight into the subject. You should make use of the brain's ability to think in images. Stories and experiences – your own, or those of others – are an excellent way to get their brain capacity to focus on constructing mental images instead of looking at you. Say or show something that arouses their curiosity. Then you will attract their attention and they will remember what you said too.

To give you an example, I started this book with the story of Janne, the gentleman with the scar across his face. Do you remember him? I think you might even remember in which decade he had his accident. Have a guess. Do you remember the transvestite Sarah Lund? You perhaps even remember the colour of her leather skirt.

Start with a story that is relevant to what you are talking about. There are different ways of doing this. I gave rhetoric training to a woman who lectured on environmentally friendly buildings. She had a rather weak rhetorical style and didn't like to be too personal. Instead, she talked in a strictly professional manner. She had to have her PowerPoint too; without it she felt as if her hands were tied behind her back. So, I realised we would have to use her slides in combination with a story. She pulled it all together brilliantly. In a rather strict setting filled with dark business suits her first slide showed Pippi Longstocking's colourful house – the yellow Villa Villekulla, with red trim and a green roof, from the children's theme park.

In that context, the listeners were taken aback, suddenly all ears. The audience wondered what would come next and, above all, how this related to what she was going to talk about. She looked at the house and started by being a bit personal, but still on a level that she felt comfortable with. "I was here with my children last summer. Perhaps you've been there with your children as well. It's such fun to see how their faces light up when they see the house. But is Villa Villekulla environmentally friendly?" With a slide and a little personal story she managed to get the audience exactly where she wanted them – to the message. Your introductory story should be an express journey that arouses interest in your message.

Strategic choice of words - Don't make yourself smart, make yourself understood

Certain lecturers are so successful not just because they are themselves on the podium and share experiences that hit their mark, but also because they make their knowledge easily accessible by using a language that everyone understands. As we've said, the consequence of talking unintelligibly is that the people who listen feel stupid, which will not help to generate that goodwill you need to create in the beginning.

So always have as your *clear communication* slogan: 'Today I won't make myself smart, I will make myself understood. That's smart!'

To avoid words that are hard to understand, go through your presentation and scan your terminology. Check to see whether you have used abbreviations or expressions that those in your profession, but perhaps not the general public, use. Such a simple thing as your title might need to be changed. What does Key Account Manager *actually* mean? A fancy title, but altogether worthless if people don't fathom what it means.

Your choice of words will affect how the listener absorbs your message. You might think that is self-evident, but it is not as common as using words strategically. Apple's Steve Jobs, who we talked about earlier, used words tactically so that customers talked about new products with the same expressions. Typical words like 'amazing', 'easy', 'really easy', 'nice', 'remarkable' and 'new'. To relatively calm, down-to-earth people it might seem rather too much to rattle off such superlatives. But Jobs and his colleagues did it nicely. And Apple does it to this day. They don't say, "The iPhone is amazing." What they say is, "What's amazing about the iPhone is…" They show something that equals 'amazing' and get the listener to use the same words.

If you use the word 'quite' in your vocabulary, then 'quite well' will also be a common assessment of how you did. If you start your presentation with the words "I shall tell you a *little* about…" the listener will say of your presentation "He talked a little about…" And there is a big difference between 'I shall tell you something exciting,' 'I shall tell you about…' and 'I shall tell you a little about…' But the important thing is not just to say it will be exciting. You must also make it exciting! Think about positive and negative words, and try to use positively charged words. Choosing strategic, positive words increases the serotonin in the brain. A negative choice of words reduces pleasure levels.

Positive words: New, lively, powerful, fast, now, simple.

Negative words: Low, afraid, miserable, shame, weak.

Vague phrasing: I think, I assume, one could perhaps, it is sort of like this, we might.

Decisive phrasing: I know, we need, I shall, it is about time that we, I can assure you that.

Avoid vague formulations and replace them with decisive phrasing. The PR strategist for the Swedish Moderate Party, Per Schlingmann, gave party members a word list – a guide to their new Moderate image – to use during the election. Here is an extract: Improve (not change), nursing assistant (not public authority employee), it should pay to work (not lower benefit levels), more people in jobs (not growth), those who earn the least (not low-income workers), diversity (not privatisation), people can decide for themselves (not choose for themselves), small businesses (not private companies), new jobs (not real jobs), people who don't have jobs (not unemployed), people (not individuals or citizens), feeling of being an outsider (not segregation).

All companies should have an internal word list so that they convey their values strategically. If you haven't got one, then it can be like it is for the Swedish Railways, SJ. They use recurring words that I consider to be far from strategic. Once I sat on a train that stood still for six hours. Every half-hour a voice announced over the loudspeaker, "Yes, as you will notice, we are standing still. We don't know why, but we should soon start moving." On another occasion I stood on the platform and waited. It was -20°c. The train was 20 minutes late and nobody wanted to miss it. So, we waited out there in the cold. The loudspeakers announced, "The train is late but it will arrive soon." An angry man on the platform shouted out, "And what the hell does *soon* mean to SJ?!" Niclas Timmerby (the managing director of YOUEP, who was nominated for the Great Speaker Prize in 2010) says that how you talk about time is something you must think about:

"What does *back soon* mean? I usually recommend that companies always communicate an exact time to show their customer that they respect their customers' time and thereby show responsibility."

Use words and expressions strategically in your presentations. And preferably define what you mean by your choice of words.

How to use a slide show presentation

First and foremost, remember that your PowerPoint is not there for your sake. It is for your listeners, it is they who should want to look at your presentation. If you intend to use it as a word-for-word script, then do a printout and put it on the table in front of you. At least then you won't have to keep your back turned to your audience.

There is a lot to say about what you should *not* do with a slide show presentation. We'll look at that quickly, and then move on to how it can be transformed from a comfort object to a really effective tool.

Slide shows should *not* be used like this:

1. They shouldn't be your manuscript. It is extremely tiresome to watch somebody read their PP while the listener reads the same text on the screen, but at a completely different pace. A presentation should be presented to the audience. If you want to reach them, it is your listeners you should look at – not what's projected on the screen. If you read aloud at the same time it will be like two people talking simultaneously – you and your PP. The audience can read themselves. Besides, our brains can't do both at the same time, which leads us to the next point.

2. You should not talk while you show the next slide, if it contains words. Let the audience read the words in peace and quiet... and then re-direct their focus back to you.

3. PP should not contain long sections or be completely full of text.

4. Don't use letters or pictures that people can't read or see.

5. Don't keep your PP turned on throughout the presentation.

6. Don't stand in front of the screen. Letters and pictures on your face are distracting.

7. Don't overload your PP with too many facts – the emphasis should not be on what is written there, but on what you say. You are much more amusing to listen to, I promise you!

8. Your PP should not surprise you – it should surprise your audience. A PP that doesn't work smoothly and surprises or confuses the speaker is tiring for the audience. They will also give the impression that you don't know what you are doing. If you are going to use your PP, you should memorize all your slides so that you know what is coming, without having to look at the pictures.

Add glimmer to your slide show

Have a look at your PowerPoint and ask yourself whether it makes you feel safe or makes you feel exalted. Your slides should be something that people *want* to look at – otherwise they are superfluous. Add what I call 'glimmer' to it – unexpected but nevertheless relevant elements that arouse interest and make the rest of the content more easy to digest.

What could your unexpected elements consist of? Think outside your area. I, as a rhetorician, try to do my best to use examples that are far from a speaker's podium; they can range from a telephone salesman to a midwife. People like it when things become a little paradoxical or 'forbidden'. The picture of Villa Villekulla that I mentioned earlier is a good example of that.

When it comes to the factual content that you must show, that information might need to be thoroughly structured. You can do it like this:

1. Compress the text into a single sentence. What is most important? What is the very essence that you want the audience to take with them? Let that remain.

2. Now reduce that sentence to a single word, or even better, a picture that summarises what you want to convey. Difficult? One word, or a single picture, can't summarise everything in the text and that is the whole point. It shouldn't summarise anything – you should do that! The message should always come from you. And the picture, word or video clip that you show in the PP should simply provide a further dimension to what you are saying and reinforce your message.

3. Use PP sparingly. It is much more fun to listen to a person than to a buzzing apparatus. Studies even show that the buzzing sound of audio-visual equipment and the subdued lighting can make listeners feel drowsy. If you want an attentive audience, you should vary the presentation between a duet with the technology and a solo performance by – you, of course.

4. Choose a font and pictures that everyone can see. That is why the preparatory work, 'the room' that I mentioned earlier, is extremely important.

5. Show what is hard to say and what must be displayed to be understood. Figures and statistics are good on PP. The same applies when you want to make something clearer, a quote, or whatever it might be. Items that the audience simply

must not miss can be included in your PP. But remember that *less is more*.

6. Vary the PP presentation with pictures, video and sound. In that way it will be a bit more exciting and the audience will wonder what the next slide is going to be about. I usually turn on pause music when the audience are going to have a little break to stretch their legs. Music has a rhetorical effect after all, so why not include it?

7. Use the 'blank' button. If you want to direct all attention to yourself, make the screen black and stand in front of it. In that way, you steer their attention directly to you.

Far too many people hide behind the PP when in fact the real boost is to emphasize the presenter. A client said that she simply was obliged to have a slide show, otherwise she wouldn't know what to say. My advice to her was that she print out the slides so that *she* could see them (and the audience wouldn't have to). Instead, the listeners can run their mental slide show that they can design themselves. The brain thinks in images. Talk in vivid pictures and listeners will see their own uniquely appropriate slides, and no PP can beat those. See your slide show as a side-kick to your show. But it shouldn't take over and say too much, and when 'Mr PP' does talk he should do it in an imaginative, insightful, rewarding and funny way, a bit tongue-in-cheek even. Which sidekick do you want? One who is amusing, or one who's as much fun as watching paint dry? Design yours so that it gives the viewer a *wow!* feeling. Or, just skip it completely. Stop abusing PowerPoint. Use it properly!

Avoid superlatives

I've heard presentations where the speaker has used so many superlatives that the public backs away because the person is trying too hard. In other words, don't overuse superlatives. The audience will not think your presentation is good just because you say so, but because you do it well.

It is the same with feelings. Before you make a presentation you should think about which feelings you want to arouse in your audience. Do you want them to feel enthusiastic, ready for action and happy? Well then you know your goals. But you shouldn't use the words 'enthusiastic', 'ready for action' or 'happy'. You should implant the feeling itself by presenting things in such a way that they simply feel like that.

If you lose your bearings

Sometimes you can lose your bearings, but make sure you don't make a big deal of this. Have a little break and go back to your headings to find the right place. Remember that you are always several steps ahead of your listener, so you shouldn't apologise for that break; it is often pleasant for us who are listening. If you have a total blackout, you can do what I usually do. I always have a gang of relevant discussion questions that I can ask, and the audience always thinks it is fun to discuss. In that way, I buy time without losing face. For every presentation, I have perhaps ten potential discussion questions that I can choose from should I have a blackout. And I, like other professional lecturers, have perhaps three blackouts a week, but that isn't something the audience notices, thanks to my back-up questions.

Wx3 - templates for you who want to exhort people to do something!

Who?
What?
Why?

Do you want something to happen, and as soon as possible? Then you should say *who* should do it, *what* should be done, and *why* it should be done. Put those three bits of the puzzle together and the audience will get the whole picture and feel exhorted to act! Here you should, of course, use argumentation technique and all the other aids. With the help of the structure of the presentation, you should be able to answer Wx3 – who, what and why. It can be a good idea to end the whole presentation by repeating the answer to why. It is after all the exhortation to act that is the summary, and the whole point. Do it!

Px4 - templates for you who want to present a solution to a problem

Position
Problem
Possibility
Proposal

If you are going to give a presentation and are faced with a problem, the Px4 provides good structure and support to move forward. First you need to ascertain what the current situation is, so that everybody is aware of what this and that look like at the moment. When you have dealt with position, you should explain how you ended up there. What was, and is, the problem.

A lot of people want to sweep the problems under the carpet. They don't want to see them, much less talk about them. The paradox with avoiding problems is that it is an excellent way of retaining them. How many times have you solved a conflict by avoiding dealing with it? If you don't deal with uncomfortable truths, they often hang in the air and lead to tension and forced smiles. I often have cases where I turn uncooperative people cooperative by putting my finger on the domination techniques that have become a part of a company's work culture. The clients don't usually like being put through this. 'Do we have to talk about the problems, can't we focus on the solutions instead?' they often say. And that is precisely the attitude that allowed the problems and the domination techniques to sneak in, seep into the very walls and become a part of the work environment. Silence is the best friend of a problem, and the worst enemy of the solution. If nobody ever says a word, we don't discover them so easily. Bosses who are afraid of conflict are dangerous bosses, even though they don't mean to cause difficulties. They think that the workplace would become locked in a conflict situation, but in fact confronting the problem is a path to a solution. Just like the problem is a path to new possibilities and a new direction. Look at the problem to find a direction away from it. Study it properly to be able to recognise it in the future, should it turn up again. And localise it quickly before it establishes a foothold. Remember that you shouldn't point at people when you discuss problems, but at the negative phenomenon you have at the workplace. That lets people dare to approach the problem, as I mentioned earlier in the section on body language. You can point, but not at people. When you've talked about the problem, you should deal with a new direction. You should get the audience to set their sights on tomorrow and do so with great optimism.

Possibility – this is the optimistic part where you should point out the direction you are aiming for. If the problem is colleagues who use domination techniques on each other, you should show them a different work climate that you dream of. Dreams are not impossible. Don't point at people – point at solutions. Unfortunately people often try to make others feel guilty when there are problems, so be careful to avoid that trap. Point instead to a proposal that incorporates the others.

Proposal – end your presentation with a proposal that should solve the problem. If you are going to change tomorrow, you need to look at what you did earlier. Assess what led up to the current situation. Provide a solution.

Persona – emphasize a suitable aspect of your character

Emphasize what it is that makes you credible in the presentation and context. Within rhetoric this is called persona, the part of your person that you want to emphasize. When I gave rhetoric training to a boss, I helped her in detail to choose a persona for every presentation. If she needed to create closeness to her employees, she talked like a colleague and started by saying what it was like when she first started as an employee at the company. If, however, she had the decision-making role, she stepped up onto the pedestal and talked about all the other large companies she had led to success. All of this was in her person and experiences. She only needed to choose the right part, for the right presentation, on the right occasion.

If you are going to talk about how to bring up children, say that you are a parent. If you don't have any children, describe a friend's brilliant way of bringing up their children. Or talk about your mother's fantastic methods – and, well, just look at how well you've been brought up. Whoever you are. And regardless of whatever the context in which you are going to talk, it is possible to emphasize your credibility, there and then. And credibility is necessary everywhere, professionally and privately. Choose that part of your character that fits in with your message.

Ethos, logos, pathos – the model that ensures the balance between facts, credibility and feeling

By now, you know what those words mean. We can abbreviate them to E.L.P. for the sake of simplicity. This is an excellent presentation model when you want to ensure that you have a balance between facts, feelings and experience. If you know that you tend to lean more strongly towards one of these three (for example, if you are a feeling person) then the E.L.P. template is for you. You divide the presentation into three equally sized parts. One of those is for figures, statistics and facts. Then you can link it to how this could help the listener. You quite simply play up why it is important for them. And, naturally, your credibility and own experiences should not be left out. So bring up your experiences in a third of the presentation, pour out hard, cold facts in the second part and emphasize the benefits for the listener in the third. If the presentation happens to be for an audience that values logos highly, then you can end it with that part. Always end your presentation with the part that is strongest. Remember the chapter on argumentation and 'two, one, three' – medium, weak, strong. That's always a good approach for your presentation.

Myths about the art of getting people to listen

No, you shouldn't imagine your audience naked. It will distract you from what you are saying and instead you will begin to dwell on what they might look like.

No, you shouldn't concentrate on a point at the back of the room so that everybody will feel seen. Nobody will feel seen, especially not those at the sides. Walk back and forth and look at one person at a time. If it is a large audience, divide them up into sections. Even if you only look at one person in the back row, twenty others will feel seen.

No, the person who looks grumpiest is not the worst whiner. What we look like when we are listening intently means nothing. We have turned off our body language and are only using our ears. Have a look at yourself in the mirror when you are expressionless, and you will notice that you don't look overjoyed, but just the opposite. I have many times discovered that those I thought were most critical and grumpy were actually the people who listened most intently and with the most interest. But if they are sleeping then your interpretation is correct – they are asleep.

No, the people sitting with their arms folded during your presentation are not necessarily critical. Sit like that yourself, and you'll notice that it is a comfortable position. Especially if you are listening (as I described in the section on body language.)

Names

Commit names to memory and juggle them a bit. Make sure that the chosen people are sitting spread out in the room. Then you have reason to share your attention and won't risk just concentrating on one side of the room. Bill Clinton was extremely good at creating rapport with the audience. In his first presidential debate, when people asked him questions, he asked them to say their name before he answered. In that way, he got a more personal form of address. I do that all the time when I lecture. I remember the names of the people who ask questions, or I mention some happy souls in the lecture if I remember their names. Then the presentation stops being a monologue and becomes communication (*communicare*, I do something that is shared).

Chronology - the template that takes the listener from pessimism to optimism

Yesterday
Today
Tomorrow

When I carried out rhetoric training at a company with a 110-year history in its field, the client wanted me to argue that change was good. Some of his employees had been chanting the mantra, 'Things were better in the old days', and that seemed to echo through the corridors like people speaking in tongues. The client wanted an inspiring half-day course. So I chose the chronological model as a solution to the problem. I asked the client to send me several covers from the long-running company newspaper. These front pages served as a connecting feature throughout the presentation. These covers varied in tone and mood, and it was hard to imagine that they were from the same newspaper. The oldest staff at the newspaper pedagogically pointed out for their colleagues that the paper has always been 'contemporary'. That it had been their anchor in the market. Strangely, the same staff members were the most pessimistic about change. Their younger colleagues were working hard and wanted to re-design the paper so that it wouldn't risk dying out with the existing, aging subscribers. But the old guard were against change. And their argument was – you guessed it – that it was better in the old days. "We have always managed to survive!" they said meaningfully to the others. But now there was a crisis. The paper was not evolving and the number of readers was decreasing.

"Interesting, you've always been contemporary and dared to make changes. That's what you've done before," I answered, and that generated a wave of facial expressions through the room. The only ones with their mouths open were the pessimists, the ones who had been most against change even though change had been what they had done before. So with my central thread I indirectly told them: "You changed yesterday, you are changing today and that is why you will still be in the market tomorrow. It wasn't better in the old days. It can be that way now as well, if you continue to change and adapt."

Improvisation (*kairos*)

Preparing yourself and using templates is a good idea, but now I want to give you what is perhaps the most important advice of all. You shouldn't just be prepared. You should also be ready to jump on an opportunity and seize the moment, just like Martin Luther King did. Or catch the spontaneous thought that turns up – right then, the second it occurs. Never be a slave to your well-prepared presentation. Should it happen to be wrong, and you think of something better when you are there, use that new idea. Magic often arises on unique occasions and at spontaneous moments. But don't misunderstand me, during a presentation you should not suddenly announce, "Shit, now I don't know what to say so I'll just improvise!" That will simply make the listener angry. Improvise, by all means, but it shouldn't be too obvious. To succeed in catching their attention, you need to gauge the 'weather' in the room (*kairos* means weather in ancient Greek and is about finding the right moment). Don't chain yourself to your planned presentation, but be with the audience. Dare to improvise and use *kairos*. But do not – I repeat, DO NOT! – let the audience know that you are improvising. That is when the magic and that *wow* feeling begin to fill the room. If you suddenly notice that the audience is looking open-mouthed at you and leaning forwards in their seats during your presentation, then give them more of it. Improvise. And go into more detail where the audience reacts and seems to want you to do so. Tell them more, provide more examples, or ask them to contribute. Perhaps they have some examples that can make your next presentation even more amusing.

Difficult types

I wish I could save you from difficult types, but regrettably they are always there. There's often at least one in every context. Some people claim that these difficult types choose special places in the room. Such generalisations are dangerous. They can make you feel aggressive towards a person who in actual fact is pleasant, but who just happened to sit where a hobby rhetorician says that stupid people 'generally' sit. So forget it. Focus instead on how you should handle difficult types neatly, without it distracting too much from your presentation. In my first book, *Domination Technique*, I write more about this. But I will give you some effective tips for tackling unpleasant types in a neat way during presentations.

If you want to ensure that people don't ask lots of questions during the presentation, you can say something, in two different ways. But remember to respect all questions that – despite your safeguards – might crop up.

1. 'If you have any questions, you are welcome to ask them *after* the presentation.' It is important that you emphasize 'after' properly, while smiling. Otherwise it might be seen as a threat.

2. 'If anyone wants to *interrupt* with a question during my presentation, then do so.' Here too it is important to emphasize 'interrupt', because nobody wants to disturb you. Then you have articulated that they can ask questions, but at the same time implanted the feeling that it is extremely wrong. You've done it subtly, but effectively, if you know that the audience is exceptionally questioning and critical.

If, however, you are a person who likes to take questions and to have an active dialogue, you can say instead, "If you have any questions, or if you think that something I have said is unclear, you are *most welcome* to ask questions during the presentation."

Sometimes, difficult types ask stupid questions to offend you and show that you are incapacitated and incompetent. This happened to Ida, one of our rhetoric consultants at Snacka Snyggt. During an evening lecture, one of the participants thought that the subject of body language was superfluous. "You can't be serious when you say that body language is so important," he said, and grinned at Ida. This person had had an aggressive attitude throughout the course. He had systematically asked stupid questions that questioned Ida's competence. She could have become really angry. But instead she chose to be professional. She turned towards the man and gave him a scenario: "There is a notice board and a moving image, perhaps a TV, next to each other. Which of these two catch your interest?"

The man, somewhat surprised, answered, "The moving image?" to which Ida replied, "Precisely." She could then continue without further disturbance.

Because Ida didn't become angry, the other participants sympathised with her. Never sink to the level of these difficult people. If such a person asks stupid questions, you can simply say, "I'll take that question with me, but for the moment I must continue," or "I can't answer right now, but we can sort this out after the presentation." If the question is exceptionally stupid, and perhaps nasty, then you can ask something like, "Where do you want to go with that question?" or "What do you mean by that?" But don't give the difficult type too much room to manoeuvre. Establish your boundaries and say, "Out of respect for the others, I must go on with the presentation so that I don't run out of time. You'll have to e-mail me if you have anything more to add."

The partes orationis model - for you who want to make a thorough job of the presentation

A simple template to keep in mind when you are going to give a presentation or speech is the *partes orationis* model. We can abbreviate all the elements in the model: IIDEMA (starting with a double i) to help you remember it. Say it a few times to yourself i-i-d-e-m-a, iidema (articulate the long i). Now that you remember the abbreviation, I shall explain what the letters stand for. I will include modern alternatives to the words in brackets.

Intellectio (analyse) – to remember this, you can link it to intellect. You should simply create a picture of the presentation situation. What is the purpose of the presentation? Who will be coming to hear it? What do they think of you and the subject you are going to talk about? Brainstorm around the situation so that you will find it easier to keep within boundaries when the job starts.

Inventio (invent) – here you write down everything you want to say in the presentation. Writing it all down might sound like too much work, but that is how you will acquire distance from what you want to say. And you can make sure the message is made relevant for the recipient whose main concern is 'what's in it for me?' Make sure that the presentation sells itself from the very start. Make it attractive for the recipient.

Dispositio (arrange) – here you should arrange the presentation in an order that is going to work. I'll deal with what that order should look like a bit further on in this chapter.

Elecutio (formulate) – Think of the word 'eloquent'. This is about the formulations and choice of words you decide on for the presentation. Make sure you choose words and formulations that people understand. Don't try to be smart – try to be understood. Remember to embellish your presentation with a strategic choice of words that will resonate with the listener.

Memoria (memorise) – In a presentation it is important that you have memorised the content. So skip the idea of reading from a manuscript, which makes you less credible. Don't read from your PowerPoint either, if you are using one. Learn the whole presentation by heart. Then the listeners will think the words come from you, and not from your PowerPoint or your script. This is self-evident. It is more entertaining to listen to a person who is talking to the audience than to their PowerPoint.

Actio (deliver) – Practise your delivery. Practise giving your presentation in front of a mirror. Don't let the occasion of the actual presentation be the first time you give it. The written word sounds different when you actually speak it, so it is important that you hear yourself articulate the words. Test some expressions and try out your body language. For an optimal presentation you might even need to have done full-blown test runs numerous times before the actual presentation. Then the words will flow naturally and you will feel so confident that you will be able to gauge the atmosphere (*kairos*), make use of it and improvise. Then you will be at your best!

IIDEMA! Now you shall arrange the presentation. As I mentioned earlier in the book, the introduction (*exordium*) is important! So the focus in the *exordium* should be to create goodwill, curiosity and credibility as quickly as possible. Example: "It's great to see you all [big smile and look everyone in the eye]. I managed to get an unpopular managing director to give a very well received presentation to her staff, who otherwise couldn't stand her. I did that with the help of rhetoric, and today you shall learn how it is done."

You don't need to use more sentences than that. After you have said this, the audience will most often want the background to the entire presentation – the story (*narratio*) – which will get them to actively listen and make them genuinely interested. Make sure that the story is linked to the point of the whole presentation. And make it as interesting as possible for the listener. Storytelling is a sort of mental PowerPoint. And it is much better too. The listener does not need to look at somebody else's pictures but can create their own mental images on the basis of what you say. *Narratio* is effective since the brain thinks in images.

This can be some consolation for you who are afraid of standing in front of people and talking. As soon as you give the listeners a story, you sort of disappear and they admire their own mental images of what you are saying. Make the story really interesting without PowerPoint – put your effort into creating mental points. And speaking of points, that is the next part of the arrangement.

Propositio – Your proposal! The story that should lead up to your proposal. Your thesis, the whole point for why the audience should listen to you. The proposal should be brief and easy to understand. For example, 'Why you ought to do rhetoric training once a year.'

Argumentatio – A thesis is sent out but it doesn't *reach into* the listener unless it includes three arguments that are as clear as a bell. I mentioned this in the E.L.P template, but it is worth mentioning again. Give the audience three strong arguments that you use in the order two, one, three – medium, weak, strong. Thus, you end with the strongest argument, the one that leaves the aftertaste. But should you, for example, find yourself short of time, start with the strongest so that it doesn't disappear if time runs out.

Refutatio – The argument from hell. I took up this point in the chapter on argumentation techniques. What is the worst counter-argument you could imagine? The strongest argument against your thesis? Name that, and sink it straight away! In that way, you show the audience that you have actually thought about counter-arguments and have the ability to change perspective.

It will be evident that you are a person who has heard weighty arguments against your thesis, considered them, but discovered that they were not weighty enough. So formulate your *refutatio* as a rhetorical question – a question that you yourself give the answer to. Then it will be like you are quoting your worst critic, and giving them an answer.

Recapitulatio – Reiterate what you said before you shot down the question from hell. We don't want that hellish question to be the last thing the audience remembers, so it is a good idea to briefly recap what you said earlier. Summarise it and then proceed to the conclusion of the presentation (*peroration*). This should appeal to the listener's emotions. The presentation should not only be given, it should make its way into the listeners' hearts. So an appeal to the listener's emotions is a good ending.

Reflect and improve

After all presentations, I want you to be your own rhetoric consultant for about ten minutes. Sit down somewhere quiet and re-play mentally the presentation you have just given. Was it good overall, which new items can you include next time and what can you do better? After having reflected on your latest presentation, you should now do a ten-times-better presentation – mentally. So if you had the chance to stand back up in front of an audience and give a revised presentation in ten minutes from now, what would you do differently? Imagine that, and then turn it into reality next time. In that way, you will never stop developing. These are ten well-invested minutes that will make a great difference in the future.

The seven-step model from Antiquity

My colleague, Barbro Fällman, has translated the following argumentation model from a Latin textbook on rhetoric:

Introduction
Hard facts
Counter argument (*refutatio*)
Concrete arguments
Solution
Consequence of the solution/effect
Conclusion

All the presentation models we've looked at in this book can be used for various types of presentations. So I won't explain this last model. Test it on your next presentation and see if it, or any of the others, work better. But now you have the tools that increase the likelihood that the audience will leave with a wow feeling after your presentation.

Three ingredients that are good to include in speeches/presentations

When the Roman orator and author Cicero lived (106-42 BC), there were no PowerPoint presentations. But his advice on what a good speech or presentation should consist of is still just as effective today as it was then. He claimed that three ingredients that I mentioned earlier in this book are necessary. A speech should move (*movere*), teach (*docere*) and please (*delectare*) the listeners. Try to always have that ambition when you give a presentation or a speech. Cicero said that it was the orator's duty (*officia oratius*). So fulfil your duty and move, teach and please with nice talk!

Chapter

10

The art of saying awkward things nicely

The art of saying awkward things nicely

"Speak when you are angry and you will make the best speech you'll ever regret." – Laurence J. Peter, North American pedagogue. Author of *The Peter Principle*

The awkward message is the one that many people delay delivering. And the longer you wait, the harder the message lands. Difficult things also steal time and energy. The ironic thing about a fear of conflict is that when you don't deal with a conflict you preserve it, and the only person who knows about the conflict is the person who is afraid of conflicts.

Before you tackle a conflict it is important to know whether it is worth it or not. Does the difficult person or situation steal a lot of energy from you and others? If the answer is yes, you should definitely read this chapter. But choose your battles. A lot of people would benefit from just letting things slide off them – the Teflon approach. Everything isn't worth a battle. But nor can everything just slide off or be swept under the carpet. So first ask yourself the questions:

What would it cost me/others if I tackle the conflict?
What would it cost me/others if I don't tackle the conflict?

Weigh up the cost. Perhaps you might come to the conclusion that you and others will benefit greatly if you confront a difficult person.

There are many scenarios for awkward/difficult messages, and the potential benefits of tackling a conflict are great. When you know that it is worth it, we can move on to the next part: What is your role in the situation?

David or Goliath?

In really severe situations, crisis communication expert Paul Ronge says that you should think about whether you are David or Goliath. If you are the boss and in conflict with an employee, you will automatically be Goliath. And you can't pull out all the stops because it isn't going to look sympathetic. The employee, however, is immediately the one who is fighting from below and can be regarded as a hero for their courage. So a Goliath can't say the same as a David. Thus David gets all the sympathy. How do you know whether you are a David or a Goliath? Take, for example, a middle-aged man who takes on a woman in her mid-twenties. From the point-of-view of the observer, he can't win that conflict nicely if he attacks her in an unpleasant way. He is bigger and stronger, Goliath, and should never have taken on a 'smaller, unfortunate young woman'. David, on the other hand, can really pull out all the stops. He has always been a winner, since childhood. In other words, a young woman 'is allowed' to say 'old bloke', but an older man will not get away with calling her a 'bimbo'. So always think about whether you are David or Goliath, and adapt your method of attack accordingly. To be David or Goliath doesn't automatically mean to be good or evil. The one who has the David role can absolutely be evil. He can, for example, make use of martyrdom to win sympathy. There are people who can't take professionally expressed criticism in the right way, but instead take it personally. Or a 14-year-old daughter who plays the martyr to be able to stay out as late as her friends. Or a wife who leverages martyrdom to govern her husband.

I'll describe the martyr further on in this chapter. But first we should examine various awkward/difficult messages and how we can get them to land nicely.

Three steps to handle your blunder

A horrible scenario that most of us have experienced at some time or another is to make a fool of oneself, to fail completely and miserably. Here, your thoughts can go into a tailspin and drain your energy. 'How are people going to react? Shall I say something or not?' There are many who envision horrific scenarios, which are often a hundred times worse than the actual result.

So, you can at least be sure of one thing: it won't be as bad as you imagine. On one condition – that the message does not come from someone else.

1. Admit what you've done
– say it yourself, and say it first

In June 2010, *Aftonbladet*, the Swedish evening paper, confronted Minister of Labour Sven Otto Littorin with a prostitute's claims that Littorin had bought sexual services from her. The actual confrontation was fairly painless. At first the journalist went up to a jolly Littorin at the airport. "Can we trouble you with a question?" Littorin straightened up and answered "Yes, of course." A moment later, this was followed by a row of censored statements that viewers only heard as a chain of long bleeps. But we could see Littorin's body language. It went from jolly to troubled. The person who seemed most affected was the colleague next to him, who wanted them to move on immediately. This clip was not aired until after the press conference that Littorin held the next day in Visby. At that meeting, a broken Littorin stepped forward. In a very emotional state, he explained that he was resigning: "I have just now informed the Prime Minister that I wish to be relieved from my duties as a government minister for private reasons and with immediate effect. There are three reasons for this, and the three are called Emma, Gustav and Arvid. They are my three children who have had to pay the price for my public life." (He had at the time been involved in a protracted, very messy divorce). He did not mention the accusations that *Aftonbladet* had confronted him with the previous day (the film clip had not yet been broadcast). Instead, he created a focus. He put the focus on a part of the problem, so that people would miss what was going to be made public the next day. After the press conference, the rest of the day was spent feeling sorry for Littorin (who had assumed the David role). And feeling repulsion for the nasty news media (the hulking Goliath). It was a dream scenario for one looking for short-term expressions of sympathy. But the nightmare would come the next day. The reason was that he had neither admitted nor denied that he had consorted with a prostitute. The day after the wave of sympathy, the witch-hunt began. *Aftonbladet* leaked the film clip they had recorded the day before Littorin's press conference in Visby. They had received a denial of Littorin's supposed purchase of sex, but he had not mentioned *Aftonbladet's* question at the press conference. The timing was just a bit too good for his resignation to be solely on account of the children, supposedly because of the stress of his divorce… or for whatever other reasons. Now everybody wondered about the *real* reason for Littorin's resignation. Had he used his children as a cover for his dalliance with a prostitute? Crisis communications expert Paul Ronge wrote this in his blog the same day:

> 'Well now Aftonbladet has finally gone from saying A to saying B and publishing the reason for Littorin's resignation. It could have happened earlier, but better late than never. Not least, it gives the ex-minister a chance not to be crushed completely by a continually worsening storm of rumours.'

The storm of rumours grew all the stronger, and that is your worst enemy when others suspect that you have done something wrong. The only way to save yourself is to lay your your cards on the table. Each day that passed, the rumours grew worse and worse. But Littorin went underground and didn't give any answers. The imbroglio worsened. From right to left it was claimed that Littorin was innocent. What proof did Aftonbladet have? His silence, some said. Silence speaks, and what it says depends entirely on the listener. In this case a response from Littorin would have been golden. Instead, he was crushed by the rumours.

There are well-known examples of people who have recognized the danger of rumours and, given the alternative, decided to offer up a confession.

On Thursday, 2 October, 2009, David Letterman shocked his audience by making a confession in front of his huge television audience. As we mentioned previously, he'd had sex with several of his female employees. In this case, he was Goliath and the female colleagues David. The reason that he confessed was that there was a risk it was going to be made public. He and his advisors decided to convey the news themselves, to limit the damage and stop the storm of rumours. He had also been threatened and he commented on that on the *Late Show* in the following way: "It [a blackmail letter] said, 'I know that you do some terrible, terrible things and I can prove that you do these terrible things'... and sure enough what was contained in the package was proof that I do terrible, terrible things." He confessed that he had done these terrible things but he didn't reveal in any detail *what* they were. No more than that he'd had sex with members of staff. The actual confession was so magnificent that the American people demanded more. And his pathos explanation afterwards gave him even more sympathy. And in the midst of all this, the blackmailer, the person who had threatened him, became Goliath and Letterman became David, who said that he was worried about his own safety and that of his family. He had felt threatened and was forced to tell about all the unpleasant things he had done.

His confession was a stroke of genius. The first show after the confession attracted 5.7 million viewers, 36% more than the week before. If Goliath plays his cards right, he can gain people's sympathy and become David.

A lot of people believe the opposite, that the troublesome message will have devastating effects. And it will if it comes from somebody else. So you should say it yourself. In 1966 the then leader of the Left Party, Gudrun Schyman, publicly announced that she was an alcoholic and was admitting herself to a treatment clinic. Two years later, she led the party to historically high election figures: 12% of the vote.

A catastrophic piece of news can be turned into a success if you have the conscience and courage to reveal it. The conclusion to draw from this is: always say it first and say it yourself. You will have a tough time ahead of you, but it can't be compared to what the speculation of others would do to you. If you confess too late, it often is quite simply *too late*.

> *"'I didn't lie, I just said something that later turned out to be untrue."* – Richard Nixon

Don't do what Nixon did; say it instead.

2. Show understanding for the shocked feelings of others

Now you have done something brave. You have let your blunder become known. But don't expect that the other person shall jump for joy when you do. Now it's time for others to react to your blunder, and the best thing you can do then is to show understanding. That might sound self-evident, but in fact it is something that people rarely make use of strategically to solve a conflict. Think about situations where you would have needed understanding instead of an explanation. A friend you are going to meet might arrive 20 minutes late and give you an explanation that takes as long again. Instead, with 20 seconds worth of understanding and an apology, the whole thing would be forgotten. Sometimes people need to meet in the understanding.

You are sitting in the hospital waiting room with ten others, in need of medical care. You have waited for five hours and at regular intervals gone up to the counter and talked with a resolute nurse. Why is she so resolute? Because she is doing everything she can, but still is faced with an angry patient. A little understanding would help 'untie the knot' and make you less troubled. Neither of you understands why the other person doesn't understand.

You go to a clothes shop where you'd bought a pair of trousers that turned out to be the wrong size. You wore them a whole (uncomfortable) evening only to discover that they were just not right. You go back to the shop to humbly ask them if you can return the trousers. The shop assistant says in a serious tone that it won't be possible. The message would have landed better if you had been shown a little understanding of her position first.

In the service industry, shops, the public sector and private relations, the whole thing about understanding is not given enough attention. I don't even know whether they use the word when they have had an unsuccessful conversation. A common question to a friend who has had a row ought to be, "Did you show any understanding?' If a tense situation has arisen, then it is most often because somebody is not sufficiently accommodating. I talked with a nurse about this and she said that she became extremely tense when angry patients came to the counter and demanded that the staff work quicker.

"I tell them that we are doing everything we can," she said, "and then I become rather irritated because they are cutting down on everything at the hospital, and yet people expect that we should be able to deal with all the extra work. But the patients don't know that."

She went on to say that she always answers, "We're doing everything we can!" Yet, that most often makes the patients angrier. There is a reason – she doesn't show understanding *before* she gives her explanation. If she switched the order it would make a big difference.

Start by responding to the person's feelings and then explain what you are doing about them: "I understand that it is extremely frustrating to sit here and wait. I'd be angry if I was in your shoes. But I promise you that we are making an 100% effort, despite the fact that we're undermanned, to ensure you won't have to wait much longer." Saying this and looking the patient in the eye should prove extremely effective. You show that you see and understand the person. You might not get an overjoyed patient who bounces back to their seat with a spring in their step, but you will get a less tiresome person. The same with the man in the shop who wanted to change the wrong-sized trousers. He might not be entitled to do that – he's already worn them for a night on the town. But a resolute shop assistant does not cheer anybody up. Say instead, "That was really bad luck that you bought the wrong size. I understand that it must be very irritating. However much I'd like to help you, the shop can't take the trousers back once they have been worn. I'm sorry about that, but I hope you understand." He will understand – at least more than he would have otherwise – for the simple reason that you understood first. People ought to think more along these lines. When the person enters the shop, office or hospital, it should feel good and safe. But it should also feel the same when they leave, even though they might not have come away with what they wanted. And the same applies when it comes to individuals. Or you. It's not only the first impression that is important, but also the feeling people have afterwards, when they've left you. How do you want people to feel when they have spoken to you? Make sure they are left with a good feeling even if you might have had to say something awkward. Combine the awkward message with understanding and sympathy, and chances are you will convey it nicely. Think about this, and test understanding the next time you find yourself in a tricky situation... and it doesn't only apply to blunders.

3.   "Sorry!"
- a good conclusion to a blunder

When you have confessed and shown understanding, an apology is a good conclusion so that you can move on and devote your energy to something else. If you have shown a healthy dose of understanding, then your apology needn't take long.

Sorry is an underrated word. Yet there are many people who do exactly the opposite after they've behaved like assholes.

Let's try something. We shall pretend that you are the person who has made a fool of themselves. You have systematically frozen a colleague out and laughed at her when she tried to join in. A really bad way to deal with the ensuing conversation could look like this:

"Why do you laugh at me as soon as I try to join in?"
"I don't think I laugh at you."
"I get the feeling that you do."
"Well, that's your own feeling. I can't be responsible for that."

As I will discuss further on in this book, criticism is bad information about you – to you. If you deal with criticism in this way, you will end up with people talking drivel about you. And, as long as you don't take criticism well, the drivel will continue. A less damaging example, but still not a really good situation, is to handle the conversation like this:

"Why do you laugh at me as soon as I try to join in?"
"I was thinking of something amusing, it just happened."
"It makes me angry."
"Listen, I was thinking of something amusing. It just happened."

The defence statement partly works, but doesn't go far enough. The goal is to get rid of the unpleasantness. And to do that you must have a rhetorical strategy. The listener is not going to drop the picture of you as an inconsiderate asshole until you have apologized. So shorten the suffering, and apologize quickly. But don't only do that – also mention the blunder the criticism is about. When she hears you do that, it will be easier for her to drop the subject.

"Why do you laugh at me as soon as I try to join in?"
"I don't really know..."
"It makes me angry."

"I didn't realize I was doing that, but I understand that it makes you angry. I apologize, and it won't happen again. I'm terribly sorry."

Isn't this going too far? Not if you compare it with the consequences of people talking drivel about you. That can be much worse. When many Swedes who'd been travelling abroad were affected by the 2004 tsunami catastrophe in Thailand, the media and the Swedish people looked for the faulty link. Why were they subsequently stranded there, and why was it handled so badly by the government, not least Laila Freivalds, the Minister of Foreign Affairs? A petition was even started: 'Give Freivalds the sack now!' Nobody dared to confess or apologize because they probably thought that the media were out to lynch them. But that wasn't the case; the affected families wanted an explanation, they wanted understanding and they wanted an apology. The main complaints were about why the government didn't arrange for injured Swedes to be evacuated and flown home. No apology was given, and the bitterness and regret linger to this day. Freivalds resigned shortly afterwards, without ever acknowledging how badly the situation was managed.

Many long, difficult conflicts with colleagues, friends and family have been perpetuated simply because a person has been too proud to say 'sorry'. It is liberating for the person who has been offended to hear that word. Even if you didn't mean any harm with your action, you can at least say you are sorry that it made the other person feel bad. The listener needs to know that you know what you have done, and that you regret it. For that reason, you should not prolong conflicts or let them take up your time, or anyone's time. Make sure you get rid of them quickly, and preferably for good, by: 1) describing your blunder; 2) expressing understanding for the person's upset feelings; 3) apologizing.

If it's a really major blunder then you should also: 4) suggest measures to repair the damage; 5) show that you are serious about your suggestion.

The art of giving criticism

Few people like the word 'criticism'. But let me define it so that you won't muddle it up with a personal attack. Criticism is related to something you do; a personal attack goes to what sort of person the other individual thinks you are. Talking about what people do should not be difficult, but since many of us confuse criticism with personal attacks we are bad at taking and giving criticism.

Perhaps you have a difficult colleague at work who for some reason makes your workday feel worse. But you can't really put your finger on why. And that is the first step: figure out what the difficulty is. And think about what you feel; is that feeling reasonable, or not? Does it come from inside you, or was it something he said or did that made you feel so uncomfortable? Once you have become clear as to what he did – for example, ignored you or smirked at something you said during a meeting – then your task is to tell him that his behaviour upset you. How do you do that? First and foremost, you pluck up the necessary courage. You can't run away from the confrontation, and you must deal with it at some point. The question is how much of your time do you want the conflict to take? Not much, right? So stand up straight and confront the person. Point out what made you upset, but avoid singling out the person. There's a big difference here. You could steer the criticism towards the person and say, "You ignored me last week." If you want to make it even worse you can throw a superlative or two into the sentence: "You bloody well ignored me last week!" But if you want it to make a soft landing, you can position the listener and yourself as equal players in the situation by saying, "It didn't feel as if we communicated so well last week." Then you've pointed to the effect of your colleague having shunned you. And now you can explore the underlying reasons together. If the person didn't think the communication was all that bad, then explain why you thought it was. At this point, of course, it will be difficult not to say 'you'. But describe it as an experience or an observation: "I noticed that you looked out the window as soon as I started to speak, and didn't re-join the conversation until I'd finished."

If, however, you can disengage a person from a mistake, then you should always replace 'you' with a passive construction. Try using 'There has been a mistake' or 'A mistake has been made' instead of 'You've made a mistake'. Naturally, the person you are talking to will conclude that she is the one who made the mistake, but the message makes a softer landing if you don't point at her.

If someone has said or done something that really hurt you, it becomes a little harder. You can't say, "Something was said that hurt me." But to help the conversation along you can skip judging the other person's intentions. Don't say, "You are mean because you said something that hurt me." Instead try something like, "What you said hurt me, and I wonder what you meant." With that you show that you are not judging the person. Instead you are describing your own experience and asking about the other person's intentions. That opens the way to a conversation, where you might otherwise have ended up in an argument. And it is not uncommon for arguments to start when a person presumes to tell you what *your* intentions were when you said or did something. That broadcasts that the person you hurt has already made up their mind that you are an asshole, and you don't get a chance to explain yourself. The result is two people with hurt feelings. So my tips when it comes to giving criticism are:

1. Don't point at the person. Point at what the person has done.
2. Express how you experienced the situation.
3. Ask what the other person meant.
4. Think about your body language and tone when you give criticism. If you look troubled, the other person will feel troubled. If you look happy, then what you say will be seen as irony. Find a balance. Give criticism in a cautious way. It is, after all, a good thing that the person will quickly come to know this, and can change their attitude. And bear in

mind which colour language you use. If you are speaking to a green, wrap up the message carefully and harmoniously. To a red, be direct, and really tell it like it is. To a blue, make sure it's well thought through and clear. To a yellow, do it pleasantly.

Many say that you should start with the compliment and end with the criticism: "You do a really good job, but you seem to do it rather slowly." The word 'but' after a compliment takes away all the pleasant charge in the praise. That's partly because of the word 'but', and partly because you end the sentence with criticism. And it is that ending that will be left with the listener as a bitter aftertaste. If you are going to include criticism and compliments all in one sentence, then do it the other way round – this defuses the criticism somewhat: "You work slowly, but do a really good job!" You can even say to someone, in a joking manner, "You're a bit crazy, you know…but really cute!" Inverting the sentence makes for an unexpected effect. The recipient doesn't really know if it was good or bad. It quite simply feels better to hear the negative words first and then get an aftertaste of something nice. That was the approach Letterman used in his on-air confession. First the unpleasant message, "I have done something terrible," and then pathos, "I am worried about my family." In that way, he retains the understanding and the sympathy. If he had said it in the opposite order it wouldn't have been nearly as effective: "I am worried about my family, and I have done something terrible." Anyhow, I recommend that you disengage the criticism from the compliments. If the criticism is matter-of-fact and objective, and points at what the person has done, then it has every chance of landing softly.

If the criticism is directed at you, it is important to have the ability to handle it. Criticism is bad information about you, directed to you. What is worse is if bad information about you is conveyed to others. And I can guarantee that the people who are bad at handling criticism can count on a lot of talk behind their backs. Just imagine how devastating it would be for a restaurant owner who serves bad food and reacts to criticism with: "OK, but perhaps you should check your taste buds because I think the food is superb." Are you going to recommend the restaurant to anybody after that? Presumably not. Will you tell them the reason why they shouldn't go there? Yep. As I said, second-hand chatter is devastating for the person who can't handle criticism. So don't shoo away honest people who express their point of view, but challenge yourself to listen quietly and thank them for their honest criticism. That could be your salvation in future situations. If you deal with criticism then it won't be spread so easily (on the condition that you use criticism to improve yourself). Criticism can be your salvation.

"The problem with most of us is that we would rather be ruined by praise than saved by criticism." – Norman Vincent Peale

How to end a relationship - nicely

Can it be done? Well, perhaps not, but it can at least be less nasty. The person who gets dumped would hardly describe it as a beautiful experience. I've experienced it. And if you had asked me, there and then, if there would have been a better way to dump me, I probably would have responded, "Yes, a much better way would have been not to dump me at all." Now, six years later, I am extremely glad that it happened. But, if I bumped into the guy again, I'd give him one piece of advice: use brutal honesty. It would have hit harder, but getting his direct, honest explanation for the break-up would have sent me further from the relationship... and on towards my new destination, which ended up being (at risk of sounding boastful here) really good.

If you are going to end a relationship, be prepared for a lot of 'But why...?!' Answer honestly and clearly. Don't fall back on the old standby, 'It isn't you, it's me.' We all know that is bullshit – it is, of course, the other way round. There are some better versions of that, for example the combination: 'It isn't you, it isn't me either – it's us.' And there might be some truth in that version – it is at least closer to the truth. Whatever the reason, don't leave your partner standing there like a big human question mark without explanation. It's tough, but if you are ending the relationship, then *do it*. Full stop.

We talked about eye contact earlier in the book. But a lot of people are cowards. Instead of looking the other person in the eye, they end a relationship by text message, by phone or via an internet chat. Or the person simply disappears for three weeks, so that the dumped partner eventually fathoms what has happened. If they do come to that realisation. I have a friend whose girl-friend stopped contacting him after they had had a rather tough patch in their relationship. My friend was deeply in love and was sure they could solve their differences. But when she disappeared, he assumed the worst. No, not that she had chosen to dump him in an ugly manner, but the very worst of all – that she had fallen into serious trouble. Since theirs had been a long-distance rela-tionship, he first desperately phoned all her friends and family. Convinced that something terrible had happened to her, he shed tears. "You don't suppose she is trying to end the relationship in an ugly manner," his sister suggested. But he was convinced: "No, she would never do that. I'll phone Interpol!" He phoned and Interpol were ready to search the country with a fine-tooth comb. They stormed in to her work place. Her colleagues were shocked, and the ex-girlfriend – who stood there behind the reception desk – was staggered. She presumably hadn't been able to imagine that an ugly break-up could take on such proportions. For my friend it was an utterly degrading experience; he was furious afterwards and never spoke to her again.

"We must talk." It's a familiar enough phrase around the world. Everybody knows what those words mean. And if you want your partner to understand quickly, you can utter those fateful words. But, I would advise you instead to see it from your partner's angle. What sort of person are they and how can the message land in the most optimal way without it turning into a total catastrophe – because that is what it will be, for them.

Expect your partner to want to ask questions. Lies might help you in the short term, but they won't help your partner. And the purpose of rhetoric, as I've said repeatedly here, is not to lie. When the truth comes out it will perhaps be awkward, but it will not be the horrific scenario you had imagined. Your partner may well be angry and shout at you. Go on explaining that you want to move on regardless of how much they shout. Or perhaps they might start appealing: "I can change my ways." Awkward, but not the horrific scenario you had imagined. If you are certain you want to move on, answer, "I know that you can change your ways, but I don't know if I can change mine – I want to move on without you. I need it to be that way tomorrow and all the days after that." It's tough, but it's the truth. And everyone deserves the truth.

"It didn't take me such a long time to get over him for one reason – he was honest," said a course participant when we talked about awkward messages. Yet another good example of what a difference direct and honest communication makes. OK, you've hurt somebody. But that is a part of life. You will certainly have been hurt yourself. And if you haven't, then no doubt 'karma' will see to it that you will be in the future. So move on! [smiley]

Dismissal and death - really difficult contexts

When it comes to giving somebody the sack, and other unpleasant situations, you can at least say it nicely. If you have to tell someone that they are losing their job, then honesty is the best policy. Tell the person they're being fired and explain why: reason-response, short and simple. It is important to be as honest and as clear as possible, and preferably in detail. The information will hurt the person's ego in the short term, but help them to do better in future employment. Don't take any shortcuts to your awkward message. Some people think that euphemisms make the awkward message land softer. But exactly the opposite is true. You extend the suffering and make it unbearable. An example of a bad alternative is this:

You: "I have something to say, and it won't be fun to hear. But I must say it nevertheless... err... have you got five minutes? Great, this might take ten, but... because there is something I must say. Don't be sad, or angry. Can you promise me you won't be? Because I must tell you something..."

By now, the other person will have had ten nervous pangs in their stomach and there will be more and more the longer you delay actually saying what you have to say. Tell it like it is, and do so straight away.

You: "I have decided not to let you stay on here, and I'm going to tell you why."

If it is an involuntary decision – if the entire company is folding – then of course you should add that you think it is extremely unfortunate. In that sort of situation, be open about what you feel. You think it is a pity? Say so. But don't try to jolly things up, with a pat on the back, a smile and the words, 'Look on the bright side, you're free!' There are, after all, dismal situations that can't be camouflaged.

Exclude any cheerfulness if it is a gloomy message. Let the glum mood be there. It is not chronic. It only needs to be there for a short time and then it can disappear. If you are the person who is delivering the unpleasant information, or you happen to find yourself in a justifiably gloomy situation, then gauge the mood and just leave it at that. You can even confirm it: "I know, it's not fair. I understand that you feel dreadful."

A good friend of mine lost her husband; he died of cancer when she was seven months pregnant. I tried to say something 'nice' the evening she texted me with the news of his death. I worked out how I could give her strength. Her lovely baby was on the way, and she had me and her family to offer her love and support. I phoned her and the answering service clicked on. While I listened to her warm and friendly voice, and heard her say their joint family name, it felt dark. She was soon going to give birth, she was 36 years old – and a widow. The information sunk in as I heard the beep, it grabbed hold of my heart and made me cry my eyes out. I wanted to be her pillar of strength and support, but all I could manage was to snivel my way through a tear-filled message about how sad I was for her. I felt like a pathetic failure who couldn't be strong for her friend. But later it transpired that, precisely because I had not sounded calm and in control, my message had been an enormous consolation for her. I had unconsciously gauged the mood and let it register without starting to talk about how she would manage because she was so strong.

In some situations, you don't need to do more than confirm that everything is a rotten mess. There are, after all, times when those jolly, *look on the bright side* types are really out of place.

Confronting someone you don't like

Should you really confront someone you don't like? Yes, and that is because of all the energy the person drains out of you... and how much energy you have to put into disliking that person, in secret. To start with, you should confront them about something concrete they've done. And by concrete I mean something he or she literally said or did. A lot of people fall into the 'he ought to twig himself' trap. But nobody's going to understand what's eating at you if you don't say something. Nobody can read your thoughts. If you confront the person instead, and give your perspective, then you can get their side of the story. Start by saying what it was that made you angry. "When I talked about my poorly father, you suddenly started laughing. You apologized, sort of, but you still kept on laughing." Now the person has a clear picture of what made you angry. Don't force a smile or laugh nervously. And make sure that your body language is in harmony with your message – you are angry at this person. Then you can ask the classic question: "What were you thinking when you behaved like that?"

There are updated versions of that question, since 'What were you *thinking*?' risks being interpreted as bullying. If you want to be more neutral and curious, you can ask, "What was that about?" Two things can happen. Either the other person explains what they meant and apologizes. Or confirms that they are a jerk by saying, or doing, something daft. But the difference is that you know which. Then you can stop wasting energy on wondering whether this person is an asshole or not – now you know, beyond a shadow of a doubt, that is the case.

Telling unhygienic types that they stink?

Can you really say that? Sometimes I wonder what people are thinking on a hot summer's day when they are standing in the metro, holding the bar above them, after apparently deciding not to use deodorant. It is rare that we actually say something in a situation like that, simply because we don't want to see that walking stink bomb embarrassed. But, the fact is that, if he perhaps isn't aware of his foul aroma, he won't have to make a fool of himself in the future if you say something now. And it needn't be so difficult if you convey the message in a light manner.

I witnessed such a scenario in a metro carriage where one young man obviously felt completely at home. He had taken off his shoes and was resting both feet on the next seat. Another young man sat two seats away and suddenly noticed the enormous stench. He turned towards the barefooted man, put his hand on his heart and said: "With all due respect to you and your feet, it's fine at home but not here. It doesn't smell good, man." The barefooted man was a little embarrassed, but not upset or angry. The other guy had after all said what needed to be said with courtesy and respect.

The event inspired me one day when I found myself next to a man on the train to Göteborg. He was really nice, and we chatted a little until he started to use his mobile phone. I sat there working on the book you are reading now, when suddenly he took off his shoes. His feet did not smell of rosebushes, and it soon became unbearable. If we had been close to our destination then I wouldn't have bothered with the confrontation. But we still had two hours to go. I thought about the young man in the metro and wondered how I should phrase it. My neighbour continued to talk on his phone and I finally wrote a message on my computer and showed it to him with an apologetic smile. Here's what it said:

> "We all of us have bad days, and today is your day. Your feet seem to have had a tough day. Would you mind putting your shoes back on? Terribly sorry to have to say this! With the best of intentions – Elaine."

He didn't look pleased, but he put his shoes back on and I could thankfully breathe fresh air for the next two hours of the journey. So my advice is: say it, but say it with respect and understanding. If it is an elderly person who for various reasons can't take care of themselves, or doesn't have anyone who can help them, you perhaps shouldn't say anything at all. Like an acquaintance, Sofia, once said: "It isn't a stranger's or a colleague's job to tell someone that they smell bad, it is the job of close family and friends to do that." I share that opinion.

Explaining to a friend that they 'haven't got a clue'

What I shall tell you now is a bit personal. When I started studying rhetoric, I was an enthusiastic member of a Pentecostal congregation. I had lost contact with a relative, and that really upset me and made me start to think about God. I read the *Bible* through to the very last page and felt that Christianity was really good stuff! I sought out various churches in the belief that I would meet lovely types, some sort of 'Jesus people', who were good and kind. When I had to write a major course essay I chose the grandiose title, 'God Exists!' Since that was a bit over the top, my fantastic teacher, Maria W. Söderberg, proposed that I instead should examine the proof of the existence of God.

'Is there proof of His existence? Hallelujah!' I thought, wanting to contribute to everyone's salvation by bestowing better knowledge through my essay. And *my* salvation was my academic advisor, José Luis Ramírez. When I prattled on about God, the pastor and my congregation, José was interested and asked questions. But, with each question, I felt more and more sceptical as to my own statements. The method José used is called *maieutics*, but more commonly known as the Socratic Method. It is a conversational process whereby somebody asks the right questions with the aim of 'giving birth' to knowledge for the other person. It is, as I have said before, one thing to send out a message, and another thing entirely for that message to be received and understood. José could easily have said, "You've become a fanatical Christian and a member of a cult." But troublesome messages 'land' better if the listener arrives at the right conclusion themselves after being asked wise, well thought-out questions. When José and I talked, I sometimes quoted the pastor more often than the *Bible*. "Is it the pastor's words or God's words that are the most important for you?' Joe would ask. He asked such questions as though he were curious to know, despite his already knowing the answer. And that made me think.

Without being aware of it, I started to examine what my faith was built upon. Slowly, but surely, I discovered that it was rooted in the congregation. And I didn't want it to be like that. I left the congregation and found a faith of my own – one that genuinely favoured me and not the congregation's interest in making a profit. When the congregation went bankrupt, many of its members lost their faith. I have José to thank that it didn't happen to me. He didn't make me an atheist, but he taught me to think critically about others, and about myself. He implanted an insight. And he did so by asking questions. So, if you have a friend who perhaps is stuck in a bad relationship, ask them what their ideal relationship looks like, and if they can think freely and objectively about it. Then ask them about the similarities between their existing relationship and the ideal. They will soon come to see that there aren't any similarities and discover that their own relationship is dreadful. Not because you have said so, but because you planted the thought by asking the right questions.

We have Socrates to thank for a good and humble method for giving birth to knowledge – *maieutics*.

The martyr method - a domination technique

I shall conclude this chapter by mentioning a domination technique that can be hard to handle when you, for example, want to give criticism. It is extremely common and if I had written *Domination Techniques* in 2007 I would have added 'The Martyr Method'. If a black person doesn't get a job at Volvo and without any grounds accuses the company of being racist, then that person is using martyrdom and his David role to try and sink the great carmaker. You shouldn't underestimate martyrdom. It is a powerful and ugly domination technique. And it can mean that a nasty David (and there certainly are some) will get away with it. You will certainly have met the martyrs at work, at home, or perhaps even among your friends. They find excuses to make themselves victims in all situations. The sun is shining today so it is bound to be rainy tomorrow. But above all, they use their 'inferior position' to gain the superior position. If something goes against them, they play this card to appear as the ones who have been unfairly treated. I'll share with you two examples I got from a client.

> "What I personally experience as tiresome is that one can't have a discussion on a professional level without it quickly becoming personal. Some people say that one shouldn't devote one's time to a person who sucks up energy, but what can one do when that is the salesman who sells the most?"

Even if the martyr is the person who sells the most, the company will lose out if it retains employees who break down their fellow workers mentally. It is self-evident that if you don't feel good, you don't do a good job either. The martyr-dominant appeals to colleagues' consciences and makes them feel that they have attacked on a personal level when really they have simply been professional. This leads to people feeling bad in their workplaces. It isn't as easy to see how many of them are out there as it is to see their stellar sales figures, but they're out there.

> "X thinks that he alone cares about the company and our customers, and that he solves their problems and he immediately takes offence when we 'accuse' him of causing confusion in the projects and says: 'It is the others who don't do their job and now I must shoulder their responsibilities too.' My analysis is that he inadvertently causes more problems than he solves in these situations, but when we try to discuss this he gets so angry and takes it so personally that on some occasions he has left the room. He takes everything personally and you can't reason with him on a professional level." – Middle manager in a large company.

A person who uses the martyr method often tries to claim that 'somebody' is out to get him or her. When you point out problems, they then claim that you are pointing at them. It is dangerous to engage in such a fight, especially if you are the Goliath in the drama. And it is important that you do it well. Say quite simply, "Every time I try to talk professionally, you take it personally. Can you restrain from doing that this time?" Alternately, "When I try to solve a problem, you react as if I was trying to set you up. That isn't so at all, and I want to assure you of that so we won't need to have this conversation in the future." Don't point at the martyr. Point at what he does and question it. If the person continues, say: "I can't discuss professional matters with somebody who takes it personally. Leave what is personal at home and then you are welcome to talk with me when you want to do so professionally."

He has a black belt in martyrdom, so let him keep it. Perhaps he is simply an extremely difficult person who doesn't need a rhetorician, but a psychologist.

Difficult people that I can't help you with

There are limits to everything. And the limit to how far I can help you deliver awkward messages nicely does not extend to people with a personality disorder. That is where the psychologists are the experts. And, if you find it hard to establish proper communication with a person, it might be because he or she has a personality disorder. These people often do not know that they have a disorder, which makes it even harder to establish contact, let alone for them to get help.

This happened to me once. I encountered a narcissist who I couldn't meet with – not because I didn't want to, but because my diary was completely full. But he tried to talk his way into an appointment. Called me a diva, but he was extremely manipulative. I managed to get him to agree to see one of my colleagues instead of me. When the colleague phoned him to find out what it was about and to book a meeting, he wouldn't say what he wanted to discuss. He insisted that she give him an appointment and meet him regardless. When she explained that we didn't work like that, he responded with unprovoked verbal abuse. I phoned his answering machine and objected strongly to his behaviour, shocked and angry that such a charming person could suddenly behave in such an insulting and nasty manner. The message I left on his machine was later played to his colleagues, who in turn mailed me and demanded an apology. The whole thing took on strange dimensions, and when I described the scenario to my good friend Stefan Söderfjäll, who has a Ph.D in psychology, he calmed me with the words, "That's a narcissist, keep well away from him."

And I kept well away. But, I want to warn you. There are certain people who are impossible to convince, to demand an apology from, or to have a decent relationship with. The psychopath and the narcissist are among these. Here is a brief description of these two so that you won't fall into the trap I did.

The psychopath: The person is eloquent, charming and manipulative, and can't handle criticism due to a lack of responsibility for their own actions. There are elements of mythomania, and the person doesn't exhibit any regret or feelings of guilt. Thus pathos does not work on psychopaths. Unless it benefits them, that is. They suffer from an empathy disorder.

The narcissist: They starts in an extremely charming and charismatic manner, but it suddenly grows and becomes uncontrolled, offensive. This person has an extreme need for self-assertion and a faulty awareness of reality. Lacks the ability to see 'the big picture' since they see everything exclusively from their own point of view. Has a great need to be in the centre, and lacks empathy. The narcissist is a control freak and in a relationship can seem dictatorial and paranoid. The need to be in control can show itself in compulsive behaviour that they themselves regards as completely natural, and where they demand obedience from those around them.

If you meet such people, I have some rhetorical advice: use body language… and run!

Bear these points in mind:

- Don't postpone the conflict – deal with it now so you can subsequently devote yourself to other things
- Think about whether you are a David or a Goliath
- Are there some awkward truths about you that risk being made public? Say them first, and say them yourself
- Don't underestimate the word 'sorry', but also refer to what you have done wrong
- Criticize by pointing at what the person has done. Don't add your own judgements about the person

- Be direct with unpleasant information – there is no reason to prolong the suffering
- If you end a relationship, you end it. Full stop
- Sometimes you have to let a bad atmosphere linger – this too shall pass
- The Socratic method 'gives birth' to knowledge for the person who hasn't a clue
- Deal with the martyr method nicely
- Beware of psychopaths and narcissists.

Chapter

11

Modern
negotiation
techniques

This chapter is called Modern Negotiation Techniques because a lot of people think that negotiation is about conquering the other person. But, as with argumentation techniques, it is actually about winning the other person over *to your side*. If you adopt that attitude, you will have a head start in the discussion. The goal is not just to get your way, but also to get the other side to understand that what you want is also good for them.

We use negotiation techniques every day, often without thinking about it. This can concern anything from travel plans with your partner to cleaning routines with your children or a salary discussion with your boss. Regardless of the situation, what I want to do in this chapter is give you perspective so that you will become aware of your own negotiation method (and that of others) and can sharpen yourself and yet still be regarded as reasonable.

How I want to be regarded as a negotiator

First and foremost, I want you to specify a goal that you as negotiator will strive to achieve. Imagine that you are a person who succeeds in convincing those around you, and think about how you want to be regarded as a negotiator.

We'll return to your goals further on. But first we must enter the jungle of negotiation techniques and concentrate on some effective methods. You might even discover that you already use some of them.

Good guy - bad guy

I'm sure you can visualise this. Two men enter a room where you are sitting with a colleague. One of them is accommodating and pleasant, while the other is brusque, irritated, critical, questions everything and refuses to look you in the eye when you are talking. The accommodating man apologizes for the unpleasant one, and the negotiation gets under way.

Or picture this: You and your partner are going to buy a new TV and you meet an enthusiastic salesman who shows you the latest models. Your partner adopts a critical role, snorts at the prices and is wary, while you apologize for him and adopt the kinder role.

One often sees this in interrogation situations in films where one person is the 'good cop' and the other the 'bad cop'.

Perhaps the most familiar classic negotiation situation involves throwing the other party a lifesaver. When one of them puts forward scandalously inadequate proposals, the other friendly negotiator sounds much better.

The friendly person's proposal might actually be so-so, but it will sound really quite good in comparison with that from the unfriendly negotiator. It is a bit like the when you are standing in a queue at the checkout in the supermarket. The bar of chocolate displayed there will have two prices – one sign will list a low, special offer price, and there will be a sign showing the normal, higher price. If the lower price had just stood on its own, it wouldn't have the same effect.

The advantage with this particular technique is that something that is only fairly decent can appear really good to the person you are negotiating with. The disadvantage is that the technique is so well known that it can seem a bit silly when used in professional situations.

In private situations it is easier. I train salesmen how to hone their selling skills, but consumers are not so sharp that the salesmen need to adopt a bad guy stance. At least not yet.

One advantage to using this technique is that it can be applied subtly. You can, for example, go alone to a negotiation as a good guy, but let someone who is not present be the bad guy.

I did that when I purchased the furniture and fittings for our office. Afterwards, my husband – with whom I run the rhetoric bureau – saw the receipt and was astounded. "You bought that much merchandise and they didn't give you a discount?" I left him with my tail between my legs and wondered if I could get a discount after the fact. Everything was already bought and paid for. But one can of course return the goods. I mailed the shop and made my husband the bad guy.

> "Hi! I would like to thank you for the lovely furniture and advice about interior decoration. I am very satisfied, but my husband almost choked on his coffee when he saw the receipt and realized that I hadn't been given a discount. 'It isn't every day that someone spends 100,000 kronor in their shop, I'm sure of that' he said. Now he is so determined that he thinks I should return everything! But I wonder whether we couldn't come to some better solution? Best wishes from Elaine."

The answer I received thanks to this technique was:

> "You have already received cushions valued at 2,500 kronor and labour costs valued at 3,180, and we also paid for all the freight costs for the fabrics, which amounted to 1,140 kronor. We have even paid for the delivery to your office, which cost 900 kronor. That means we have already deducted 7,720 kronor from the actual cost. We'd also like to include the price of the fancy lamp we looked at for the little room, which would give a further bonus (value 1,790 kronor). The total discount would then be 9,150 kronor. With best wishes, (shop manager)."

A total discount of around 10% is perfectly satisfactory, though I could almost certainly have gone further. But at this point I didn't want to steamroll them; I wanted them to also feel like winners. So, I thanked them for their offer and said that we would certainly return to them in the future, and we counted on their being just as professional and accommodating as this time.

What I made use of was not only the bad guy-good guy ploy, but also the scare rhetoric tactic that I'll describe next.

Scare rhetoric

You can use this technique to scare the other party towards your goal in various ways, with the help of subtle or obvious threats. You might try it when you're on holiday, haggling over the price of a pair of sunglasses with a seller on the beach. You name your lowest price but are given a price that you don't like. You shake your head and then take a couple of determined steps away. When the seller sees that you are serious, he calls you back and you get the price you wanted.

Or it could be the boss who uses scare tactics in a salary negotiation. In this case it is a particularly rotten trick because you are in a position of dependence. You say what you would like your salary to be, while the boss advises you that there are many competent people queuing up to take your job. You get cold feet and accept the same salary for another year.

When it comes to scare rhetoric, it is important that the frightening information you give to the other party is true, otherwise you may be asked to show your cards; if you're bluffing, you lose. You should only use this technique if the person you are negotiating with has a completely false picture of the situation. It might be the case that it is you who are the boss and you have a pompous employee – who doesn't deliver. He nonetheless demands a salary that's higher than what the most competent employee receives. You must then explain the situation to him, even though it might be frightening.

You can use this technique in your everyday life even though you might be at a disadvantage. When my husband was going to leave his former employer after 18 years to work with me, he was offered a 10-15% salary increase, versus the raise of just 3% the same company had previously offered him. Why? They were afraid of losing him. The increase was offered when he'd decided to leave, and it felt almost a bit disappointing for him.

So, before you negotiate your salary, have a look round and check with your company's competitors whether they would be interested in hiring you – and what salary they might offer. When your boss feels safe, you can show a reality that is a bit more frightening for her. But it is important that it is truthful.

The psychological consequences with the scare method can be:

Fight – The person scares you in return.

Flight – The person flees, afraid to negotiate.

Passivity – A form of indifference; the person becomes paralysed.

The team-play method

This negotiation technique should get the other party to feel that you both want the same thing – and that the grass is greener on your side of the fence. It is simply a matter of formulating every argument in such a way that it becomes attractive for the other party. When I explained this, a client said, "So, it's like telling somebody to go to hell in such a rhetorical way that the person looks forward to the journey." And one could see it like that, of course. But, since rhetoric strives to be truthful, this is not about trying to make something that is ugly look better than it is, but about pointing out the advantages in what the other party might see as disadvantages.

The downside with this method is that the other party can come to feel that what you are saying is too good to be true. So, all the arguments you put forward should not be positive. Instead, raise a counter-argument. When you want to convince somebody, have *three* arguments in favour, and *one* argument against. (You will remember that from the argumentation chapter.) Then the other person will feel that you have gone outside yourself and also seen others – you have perspective on this and that.

Think, for example, about the people who are clever at selling mobile phones, like Peter whom I wrote about earlier. First they take you to the telephone you were interested in from the start. They are not overly enthusiastic when they talk about it, but they do nevertheless mention all its advantages. When you ask what they *really* think, they'll look rather mischievous and whisper, "Don't tell my boss, but there's a phone that is much better value for money." That's when they gain your confidence, since they've shown that they have a perspective that extends *beyond* their job. You've been hooked and you buy the phone – the model they had in mind from the outset, although you were unaware of it. You gained confidence in them because they dared to say something negative about one of the products they were selling.

When something seems too good to be true, it arouses suspicion. So, when you negotiate, remember that you should not present what you are offering in *too* positive a way. Mention some negative aspect and then the other party will feel that things are starting to look more realistic. The advantage with this method is that you will learn to see and present things from all sorts of angles, things that otherwise could land badly with the person you want to convince. Let's say that you want to take your restless, high-strung friend on a getaway to a desert island. How will you get her to understand that this something that will be good for her? Or get your six-year-old son to *want* to clean his room without having to bribe him with toys? He has to understand that he will get something for the work. Think 'team-play method' and find three sharp arguments. If you can crack that nut, you can probably sell ice to an Eskimo!

The compliment method

If you've read my first book, *Domination Technique*, you will certainly recognise that the compliment method is a domination technique. It is when you flatter the other party into action. You sandwich wishes/demands/tasks between compliments to build up feelings of being in debt, a sense of guilt.

When we link a task to a compliment, it means that we put that person in debt. You expect to be thanked for the compliment. The psychology behind this is extremely simple and it is used in many contexts, for example in your supermarket. It is not out of friendliness that shops hand out free samples. Studies have shown that the principle of repayment is something that's built into us.

When we get a feeling of being in debt, we do everything we can to get rid of it. On the days the shops hand out free samples, customers buy more. We feel that we should give something back and we do that by buying more. But this, of course, happens without our being aware of it. It's the same with compliments. As soon as we get a compliment, many of us feel obliged to do something in return – either deny the compliment or do what the cleverest people do, which is to say thank you. But those who are bound by the Law of Jante say 'pah!' and pay back by fulfilling the wish/demand/task that the compliment was linked to. It is an unnecessarily high price, if you ask me.

In negotiation techniques, you can use the compliment method by bringing up advantageous qualities that the other party has made you aware that they possess. Let's say that your son presented himself as being a very thorough sort, but you find that his room is still a mess. Instead of scare rhetoric – "Get it cleaned up, now, or there will be no sweets on Saturday!" – you can use the compliment method. "Darling," you might say, "it's time to show your thorough side that you told me about." Then you've given a compliment and an exhortation that is based upon how the other party has described themselves. The alternative for the other person then becomes a dilemma: live up to what they have said or they are going to look unreliable. Few people choose the latter in negotiation situations. The same applies at your workplace. Perhaps you have a supplier who has convinced you to use their services because they are quick and efficient. If you get into a panic and really do need a delivery the following day, you phone the supplier and remind them of their image. Then they will definitely make an extra effort.

The disadvantage with the compliment method is that it does not arouse true motivation.

Give – guilt

This technique builds yet again on the principle of repayment, but there is another way there than via compliments. Instead of flattering the other party, you have prepared a mental list of everything you have done for her and it is so long that she'll feel overwhelmingly guilty and will want to repay you. This works well only on the condition that you are not sitting opposite a psychopath or a narcissist – guilty feelings are not a part of their world.

So what you are saying with this list is roughly a version of 'You scratch my back, and I'll scratch yours.' Instead you say, "I have scratched your back for many years, now it is your turn." The other party will do everything to bulk out the list of everything she's done for you. Make sure you are prepared and always have the longest list yourself.

The consequence of this method is that nobody is going to look forward to meeting you because you will be so strongly associated with guilt feelings. An example from everyday life could look like this: A friend or family member always gives you guilt feelings. When you see who is phoning you on your mobile, you get a sinking feeling in your stomach and avoid answering the call. When you do finally answer, and try to sound glad and friendly, the person says, "You never answer." He always finds a way to make you feel guilty. Since we humans basically do not want to live with guilt, we avoid such people.

If you are going to negotiate, use this method sparingly.

Which negotiation technique are you using?

So, you've now learned some proven, effective negotiation techniques, and I'll bet you even recognise yourself in some of them. Are you a person who uses scare rhetoric or the compliment method?

Let us go back to the goals that you sought to achieve as negotiator – and how you want people to see you. Do they correspond with how you act today? If not, it is time to change and behave differently. An unfortunate tendency is that we repeat old patterns regardless of whether they lead to success or not. Change your style and do things differently. The most common pitfalls that a lot of people step into are:

1. You play too tough – Goodwill is incredibly important.

2. You adopt a poker face – It is your body language that strengthens the message; don't exclude it.

3. You are uncompromising – Don't be a robot, show your human side.

4. You are too eager – If you seem desperate, the other party will make use of that.

5. You're simply too smart – You won't learn as much if you act as if you already know everything. A lot of people who do the opposite, and act as if they can't follow you, often get more information than they had expected, since they think they're too stupid anyway to be able to handle the information.

6. You go along with the bluff 'standard agreement' – It is always possible to adjust the rules even if it is a so-called standard agreement. This is the most common bluff in negotiation technique.

7. You act under pressure of time – Take a break and a deep breath. Book a new meeting. Buy thinking time. You won't make well thought-through decisions if you are pressed for time.

8. Make decisions in affect.

Here are some things that are good to bear in mind:

- Find out about the negotiation frames – What are your frames and those of the other party? If you are going to negotiate your salary it is good to know what salary you would like to have, as well as what the range of salaries is in your company. What is the highest and the lowest salary? A lot of people don't get hold of this information and put up with a rotten salary far too long, while younger colleagues who've worked there for a third of the time earn a third more.
- Put yourself in the other party's situation – Sharpen your arguments, but it is even better if you know about the other party's sharpened arguments so that you can sink them there and then.
- Set up the frame for the meeting – Make as effective use of the time as possible, and make sure you have said what you really want to have conveyed. It is important from the start that you set the frame for what you are going to talk about. The one who does that, wins.
- Give the other party a lot of alternatives – If you say 'You have two choices' the person will feel they are in a tight spot and under pressure. We don't want that. But if you put forward ten different options, it will feel like a smorgasbord of choices, but what the other party doesn't know is that these are your choices. It's similar to going to the bank to choose an investment fund for your savings, and the bank shows various alternatives that you can choose from. The catch is that you are choosing from among their picks, which are guaranteed to be good investments for the bank as well.
- Ask questions – You can never get too much information. It is best if you start the meeting by listening and asking questions. In that way you will get a better picture of their situation, what they need and what you can get from them.

So, forget the boring 20-minute presentation on the company's history. The only thing the other party is interested in is what they can get from you.

- Make use of active silence – This works particularly well on monologue monsters since they feel uncomfortable with silence and will leak involuntary information.
- Never accept the first offer – The other party will presume you're not agreeing to it. Respond instead with your unreasonable, far-fetched 'wishful thinking' offer, and you will soon meet.
- Forget prestige – Don't take it personally, take it professionally. If you don't like the other party, put your feelings aside and focus on the goal.
- Be tough when it comes to factual issues, but flexible with people.
- Win points without making enemies.
- Be a good loser – When the other party leaves the negotiating table, leave the door open in case she regrets her decision. Say, "Good luck, and remember that you are welcome back if you aren't satisfied with the others."

How to negotiate your way to a higher starting salary - nicely!

This is a negotiation situation that everybody has to deal with at some time – what will your salary be? It is your first job and your employer might well regard you as 'the young girl who should be glad to have a job'. Or you may be changing jobs, or looking for a pay rise in your existing job and are regarded as 'the older person who will surely be satisfied with a slight bump of 200 kronor more'. But the truth is that they are the ones who should be glad to have you! Let that be your starting point when you discuss your salary; that and some rhetorical tricks that you will get here.

1. What is your dream salary?

Before you go in to see the boss, you must ask yourself a few questions to stretch your own understanding of what salary might be possible. Ask yourself how much would satisfy you? Make you happy and overjoyed? Write down those three goals now:

Satisfied:
Happy:
Overjoyed:

2. Have a relaxed attitude

Instead of coming into your salary discussion with a severe position and exaggerated respect, try to find the same relaxed style as when you try to persuade a tired friend to go with you to the pub when you want an evening out. Emphasize what the benefits are for the other person – in this case your boss – instead of using the martyr argument, 'I think I deserve it'. It doesn't matter how high a salary you think you deserve. You must be able to say why. He who can talk nicest, wins. Half the secret of a successful salary discussion is to come equipped with well-prepared arguments. This is what you do:

3. Conduct research

Working through a successful product salary discussion is about being rhetorically effective. Start by finding out everything that is connected to the salary. What does the salary ladder look like? What is the spread of salaries in your company? Ask colleagues and others. What sorts of salaries do competitors pay their staff? Dig out all the facts.

4. Brainstorm arguments

Write down five arguments for why you should have a higher salary, as well as five positive things that the boss would win by giving you a raise, and five benefits to the broader company. But also write down five sharp reasons for NOT raising your salary, seen from the perspective of the boss, and what you can say to obliterate those arguments. Do your homework and you will have an enormous head start!

Why I should have a higher salary:
What the boss gains from my having a higher salary:
What the company gains from my having a higher salary:
Five compelling reasons for not giving me a higher salary:
Five good counter-arguments why I shouldn't get a higher salary:

5. Arrange your arguments properly

Divide your arguments into three parts. First set out what the workplace gains by your salary being raised, then why you deserve it. After that, you yourself should think through the 'statement from hell' – the best counter-argument your boss could potentially throw at you – and figure out how you'd shoot it down. Finally, go through what the boss himself gains by your raised salary. Now you will have prepared your case according to the principles of argumentation technique:

Medium (the workplace gains).
Weak (you gain).
Counter-argument (why you *shouldn't* get a higher salary).
Strong (the boss gains).

Now get out there and negotiate, and do it nicely!

Storytelling – giving speeches to people who want to listen

There will be occasions when you will have to give a speech. And despite the fact that you may want to give those speeches, perhaps you won't dare. With this chapter, I want to inspire you to go from being that type who says and feels, "I am not a public speaker" to become the type who stands there tall and straight and feels, "I am a public speaker." It is important that you are still yourself, regardless of whether you have to stand up in front of a group at a wedding or an office party. When it is you who's speaking then it is you – not somebody else – that we want to hear. And take your mental rhetorical room with you; it will make you calm.

Practical things that a lot of people know about, but also miss

Stand so that everybody can see you. Don't hide behind a desk or a podium. You will arouse more commitment and joy of listening if everyone can see you. It is perfectly fine to sit on a table in a relaxed pose if you feel vulnerable, but don't create distance between you and the audience. But nor should you create too much closeness. There are some people who don't sense other people's personal space and how close they may come. If you notice that somebody pulls back, then you should back a little too, but that doesn't mean you should melt into the wall.

Speak into the mic if you have a mic

Far too many speakers start by whirling it around, or letting it sink down towards their hip and then we miss everything they say. If you haven't got a mic, speak loudly enough for everyone to hear you. Ask loudly and clearly whether everyone can hear you, and if people on the back row nod affirmatively then that's OK, you can start your speech.

Look at the people you are talking to

If you think this feels creepy, there is actually a short cut. Namely, look at the person to whom the speech is addressed. You can look directly at the bride or bridegroom, if it is a wedding speech, and get your strength and courage from them. If the person you are talking about is not there, you can let an empty space next to you symbolize that person.

Stick to the time limit

You can actually say rather a lot in three minutes. That is a really good time frame for a speech, regardless of whether it is at the end of a school year, a wedding or an office party. If you are going to talk longer than that, then tell the audience so that they can prepare themselves mentally. But the risk is that they will start looking at the clock.

Do not meta-talk

A lot of people start by talking about what they are going to talk about, and about how difficult it has been for them to think of something. Others talk about feeling nervous and say things like, "Yes, well, here I am and you're sitting there…" or "I sat down and wrote the speech this morning." Skip all this meta-talk. We don't want to have the tedious background information unless of course it adds something very special to the speech. And it rarely does, so skip the talk about the talk and start talking instead!

Start with something that you (or somebody else present) actually experienced

To get people interested in your speech as quickly as possible, it can be a good idea to talk about something you, or somebody else present, experienced. Two things that usually work well are nostalgia and subjects that make people unbearably curious.

There are a few introductory phrases that arouse people's curiosity:

I have something embarrassing to tell you...
I have never told anyone this before...
What a lot of people don't know...
I have a secret that I am going to divulge...

When it comes to nostalgia, it is a good idea to start stories with hints about that and a bit of recognition. That's particularly true when you're talking to a group of people who share your frame of reference and belong to the same generation. Then it will be easier for them to create a picture of what you are talking about, since they have themselves experienced the same time and place, the same sensations and feelings. Some examples:

When I was ten years old...
My first love was...
I remember my first day at school...
When I was little I wanted to be...
In my youth I went dancing at...
I awoke to the Breakfast Club...

The contents first

Those who give a speech without hinting at the final destination and contents often lose their listeners' attention. It is important that you show clearly where you stand and where you are going when you begin your remarks. Make sure that you express this as soon as you can, preferably at the very beginning.

Those who are listening to you want to hear the point of the story first so they'll have an idea of where you are going and also have a sense of control. So think about which sentence you want them to remember from your story. If it is a speech at a student matriculation party, perhaps the sentence could be, 'Take risks, but don't be foolish'. You could then share two stories with your listeners, one where you took risks and one where you were fool-ish, so that they will understand how you came to that conclusion. If it is a speech at a wedding and you want to tell the bridegroom that he is your best friend, you should start with, "You are my best friend…" and then give examples of why he is. To start with the contents and end with the same conclusion is a neat way of tying it all together.

Don't ask people to cheer

"Are you feeling good?" a person might ask to start their speech. The idea is presumably to be polite. The problem is that they create a feeling of 'Now I must answer yes'. The audience wants most of all to just listen to your speech, not to play along with the speaker's request or start cheering – that should come spontaneously. In other words, avoid asking questions that force the public to answer.

You can, however, ask rhetorical questions – questions that you answer yourself. Then the public still feel they are safe observers, instead of feeling confronted by the speaker. Most important of all is not to test the public's knowledge by asking them what they know or don't know.

Try to make what you are talking about come to life

By doing that, the listeners will see what you see. Since body language follows thoughts, it is important that your audience concentrates on the message, never on the situation of the speech. Visualize what you are talking about. That will help to lessen your nervousness as well as make your speech more interesting.

Sad speeches

Sometimes occasions arise where your speech is going to be sad. It might be at a funeral, which people will be deeply saddened, or at a company that is going to be closed down, making thousands of people unemployed. There are two things you should bear in mind when you give a sad speech. When you talk about something unpleasant that has happened to you, you will create a feeling of bad conscience in your public – you say you feel bad and then they will want you to feel better again. Don't place that responsibility on the public, rather you should always ensure that you have a rhetorical bridge away from an unpleasant message. The other thing is to describe something positive that the event has taught you. By so doing, the public won't feel that responsibility; instead they will be able to take in and be moved by your experiences and learning.

Things that will make you comfortable

Yawning
This forces your body to relax. It is very effective when you are extremely nervous. Go into an empty room before you give your speech and have a marathon session of yawning – you will feel much calmer.

Jump around and shake off your nerves
A lecturer told me what she did to get rid of her nervousness. She jumped up and down in the Ladies and shook her head and made silly faces to loosen up her tense jaw (which are a common sign that you are nervous). Then she stood and said nice things to herself in front of the mirror.

Say nice things to yourself
Psychological studies show that we are just as influenced by what we say to ourselves as by what others say to us. So if you should happen to say to yourself that you are ugly, you will feel just as gloomy as if it had been your spouse or a stranger on the street who had said it. It is what you say to yourself in your head that triggers your nervousness. 'Hell, I'm so nervous. This is never

going to work. I'm not going to manage this. How terrible!' Those are fairly common feelings when you're nervous. Imagine that you are just about to get up and give a speech in front of your colleagues and then the boss comes past, looks at you and says, "Hell, you're so nervous. This is never going to work. You're not going to manage this. How terrible!" Most people would simply back out and never give the speech. You might think that it is something different if the boss says it, but that is exactly what it is not. Neurologically, it is exactly the same thing, and you react in the same way. So, stand in front of a mirror before your speech, look yourself in the eye and say, "You are so strong! This is going to go really well! You'll pull this off brilliantly! This is fun!" That will have just the same effect as if your boss had said it.

Pen or prompt cards

Sometimes it is hard to know what to do with your hands. I usually advise people to copy the body language they have when they talk to people they feel comfortable with. To make yourself more comfortable, you can take something with you to hold that doesn't disturb those who are listening. This could be prompt cards with some headings, or a pen – but make sure it isn't a click pen. What you take with you to the podium should make you feel safe, but it mustn't distract from what you are saying.

Focus on one friendly face, or several friendly faces, in the audience

One face is okay, but if you can find three or four faces in different places among the audience then your presence will be experienced as better. And the people close to those you look at will also feel that they have been seen. It is sufficient that you look in the direction of somebody even if you aren't looking at them in particular.

So when you are asked to give a speech at your best friend's wedding, or a student matriculation party, or some other celebration – don't let fear stop you. **Just do it!**

Chapter

12

Shit happens

At my rhetoric bureau we give training in rhetoric to – among others – people from the business world. Approximately once a month, we have open courses. Different types of people from a variety of fields come to these. Something that most of them have in common is that they feel a certain (sometimes a considerable) discomfort when it comes to speaking to an audience. And to get over that discomfort, we usually talk about what it is that feels so frightening. What is the worst that can happen? 'That you lose your thread', 'That you make a fool of yourself', 'That you forget what you were going to say' are some of the answers, and I am almost surprised that they aren't afraid that worse things could happen. My attitude tends to irritate them because 'there is nothing worse' and 'rhetorician Elaine can't have experienced that'.

A lot of people come up to me and say. "All this rhetoric stuff comes to you *naturally*", "*You* have a gift for this" and "It is easy for you to say that one can catch the attention of a large audience and get them to listen." All that, dear reader, is bullshit. I do not have a gift. I have *learned* how to get people to listen and have a university degree in Rhetoric so that I can teach others how you do it. Besides which I hold several lectures every week. Nonetheless, I still make a fool of myself, at least once a week! It feels horrible when it happens. But let's say it is my treat, and I talk about it the following day and get the entire audience to laugh with me – and at me. So to help you dare to go up onto a stage in front of an audience, or give a presentation to your company's clients, give a wedding speech in front of all the guests, or have a conversation with the person you're in love with, I shall describe some of my best (worst?) bloopers. It is my hope that you will be able to think about these and feel, 'It can't be as bad as it was for Elaine!' And then say what you want to say as nicely as possible. And if it isn't nice, you can always joke about it the next day.

A bad cold

It was a runny-nose morning and I was going to give a lecture to 2,000 businessmen in Stockholm. On my way to the event, I realised that I had forgotten my nasal spray. Well, never mind, I thought, even though my runny nose was turning into a real downpour. I stepped out of the taxi, went inside and said a cheery hi to everybody. The sound technician put my mic on, and this time it was a headset. Once up on the stage I had the public in my rhetorical grasp, they were happy, I was happy. They had just been given the task of turning to their neighbour to discuss how much rhetorical training they were given at their workplaces, when my nose simply overflowed and I – who didn't have a hanky with me – sucked in for all I was worth. The entire hall suddenly fell silent and everyone gave me a questioning look. "Did you hear that?" I asked nervously. I got a burst of laughter in return. Of course. The mic was turned on and they heard more than they wanted to.

The capital-city blooper

I was in Sweden's second biggest city, Göteborg, and an audience of about 300 people sat and listened to my lecture about domination techniques. I had talked for about two hours. They were in a good mood, curious, and they thought I was credible. I was going to give examples of how people who are bad at receiving compliments behave. So, as part of an exercise, one person got to give me a compliment that I'd written out in advance. "Elaine," she said, "you who are such a good lecturer, could you give us a lecture tomorrow afternoon?" I was meant to answer, "No, I must take the train at 12 noon and travel to Stockholm." But I heard myself say, "No, I must take the train at 12 noon and travel to Sweden." Need I add that that is the worst thing a person from Stockholm can say to 300 people from Göteborg (in Göteborg). The audience did not laugh but just rolled their eyes. Which they had every right to do.

The conversation with my new boss

I had just begun a job dealing with rhetorical issues at the PR agency Ronge Kommunikation (Now called Deportivo). I had met my new boss, Mattias Ronge, twice. A week after I had received the good news that the job was mine, I ran into Mattias a third time. I was fairly nervous, as one is when you meet your new boss. Nothing must go wrong. He sat with a mate at a café and he had his newly born daughter with him. He gave me a jolly wave and signalled that I should come across. I shyly tiptoed up to them and saw the baby.

"Oh, is she yours?" I asked, and looked at Mattias.

"Yes," he said, every inch the proud father.

"Oh she's so cute," I said, and went on, "She must look like her mother!"

Suddenly Mattias and his mate burst out laughing, but I didn't understand why. I was concentrating on making a good impression on my new boss. But guess how I felt when I realised that I had insinuated that I didn't think Mattias was much to look at. Luckily for me, he is a cool type and he didn't take offence. I, on the other hand, can still turn bright red when I think about that blunder.

The Evangelical pastor blooper

I was standing in front of staff from Skanska and was going to tell about how I once had lectured to a group of trainee Evangelical pastors. The audience sat there, all eyes, and waited for my story. But first I wanted to make sure they were familiar with the culture in Evangelical chapels. I wanted to ask whether they had been inside an Evangelical chapel, but instead I heard myself say, 'Have you ever been inside an Evangelical pastor?'

Thank God it was an audience with a sense of humour, but it was painful.

The cancer mistake

I was giving Lotta Gray (*Vimmelmamman* – the Bewildered Mum) some rhetorical coaching before a lecture she was going to give. Lotta, as I mentioned in the chapter on blog rhetoric, is the author of a blog that has 55,000 readers a week. She writes about what it is like to live with cancer. She was thinking of acquiring a web page for her lecturer profile. I wanted to tell her how simple it was to get clients to choose her instead of speaker agencies. "Just put your booking assistant's e-mail address on the page," I said, and showed her my page with contact details. It said:

> *Mobile phones can give you tumours,*
> *An email can give you an answer*

I wanted to disappear into thin air when I saw my cheeky sub-heading. I apologised profusely and explained that I was mortally embarrassed. Lotta took it very well and mainly laughed at how incredibly embarrassed I had been.

The open zip blooper

I remember one seminar where I began my introduction with the zip of my trousers wide open, without my knowing it. The audience seemed unusually uncomfortable. A woman right at the front pointed it out after ten minutes. I began to sweat, but then I had a brainstorm that might save me.

I asked the audience how many of them had noticed my open zip. There were 70 people looking back at me and just as many hands went up. Afterwards this was followed by a lot of hearty 'poor little dear' laughs, because they were a friendly crowd. "Okay, keep your hands up. Now we will see the strength of words compared to clothes. I said in my introduction what my company was called. Do you remember that?" All the hands dropped down. "Not so strong. Now you know how important clothing is when you want to deliver a message. It can strengthen, weaken, or as happened in my case, completely eclipse what you actually say," I said and pulled the zip up. To my audience I looked like a cheeky type. But deep inside I felt absolutely awful. It didn't get any better when someone came up to me afterwards and with a very slow and pedagogical tempo said:

"Elaine...having your zip undone like that... to sort of... make a point... don't you think that was going a bit too far?!"

Of course, they were right. But that wasn't what it looked like. Even six years after that incident I am still traumatized by it and now always wear tops that cover the zip. I want to guard myself against the fact that, well, 'shit happens'. The same thing needn't happen twice.

Conclusion

Be the best version of yourself

And, so, you and I have come to the end of this book. We started with Janne, with the scar on his face, made a journey through rhetoric to get people to listen to you and concluded with 'shit happens'. Now all you have to do is go out and practise. Don't be frightened if you make a fool of yourself at times; you can turn those occasions into amusing stories in the future. You have now read a book about modern rhetoric and I want you to remember something important. Namely, those who practise, improve. Those who don't, don't.

When I coach my clients in rhetoric, we have 50% exercises and 50% theory. Some of the exercises have been described in these pages. Practise as much as you can. I think that old Chinese proverb is really very accurate: 'I hear and I forget, I see and I remember, I do and I understand.' So, do your rhetorical training once a week. It isn't difficult since you already talk to people many times a day. Just try to talk nicely.

Yet again, I want to remind you that you won't necessarily be a Barack Obama or a Martin Luther King. You can, however, study role models in your field, or in other contexts where you want to be listened to. Studying other people's rhetoric can be the best lesson for your own commentary. But your training comes from testing what you have studied.

The old cliché, 'Be yourself, everyone else is already taken', is so true. But I want to take that further. The goal of talking nicely is that you should be the best version of yourself. And you will be that best version most often if you talk with people you feel comfortable with. That is the art of talking nicely.

I studied my sister-in-law Hanna during a family dinner. She said she wanted to take a course in rhetoric so that she would dare stand in front of an audience and get them to *want* to listen to her. I was rather surprised and wondered why. When she sat there talking with the family she did it so graphically, gesticulating and getting all around her to laugh and listen with interest. She was at that moment the best version of herself and that is exactly what I want to achieve. The most brilliant communicators are not more remarkable than that they succeed in being themselves in front of large numbers of other people – that is the secret. The goal is that you should now be able to have conversations, give presentations and speeches and take part in awkward discussions, the same way that you would have done in front of a small cluster of people you like. That is when you are most relaxed, inspire confidence and are amusing. Study the jargon you use with your friends and take it with you to other occasions. Try to be yourself in front of all the other people. And remember, "It always seems impossible until it's done." (Nelson Mandela)

I wish you a big 'Good luck!'

An introduction to
Elaine Eksvärd

Elaine Eskavrd is the CEO and Founder of rhetroic agency, Snacka Snyggt, that offers a variety of courses in modern rhetoric, presentation techniques and sales rhetoric. She is a Swedish TV personality and an avid blogger writing about family life, rhetoric, relationships and fitness.